HOW GOD REVEALS HIS LOVE IN

A FAX FROM HEAVEN

AND OTHER TRUE STORIES

FAYE ALDRIDGE

Published by Davis Jackson Publishers
Mt. Juliet, Tennessee 37122
www.DavisJacksonPublishers.com

All Scripture quotations noted are from the King James Version of the Holy Bible, (Public Domain)

Library of Congress control number 2009912357
ISBN: 978-0-578-04313-5

Manuscript written by Faye Aldridge
Editor: Brenda Noel
Designer: Alison Griffin, www.amGriffinDesign.com
Cover Photos: ©iStockPhoto.com/Wong Chee Yen
            ©iStockPhoto.com/DianeLabombarbe
Back Cover Photo: Donna Layne
Interior Photo (rose): Alison Griffin
Interior Photo (crown): Bruce Watkins
Interior Photo (shrapnel): Jacob Layne

Printed and bound in the U.S.A.

Dedication

To my Heavenly Father,

Donna and David,

Jacob, Daniel and Reese,

and

in loving memory

to

~ Burke Aldridge ~

Because I love you all.

Acknowledgements

To Dr. Carl Willis and Dr. Arthur Cushman, who made me aware of their amazing encounters with my deceased husband, Burke Aldridge, I acknowledge my gratitude. To each of the people whose stories appear on the pages of this book, I am grateful to you for opening your lives so that others might be encouraged and receive hope by reading about your experiences.

I offer my sincere thanks to Lewis M. Lamberth, Jr., Director of Pastoral Services and Baptist Hospital in Nashville for their assistance and cooperation during my quest for credible people willing to share incredible experiences.

To my editor, Brenda Noel, who pushed with grace, whose editing expertise made correction bearable, I thank you for helping me turn *A Fax From Heaven* into a reality! A special thanks to Alison Griffin for the graphic design of the cover and interior layout of the book.

I would like to acknowledge and offer thanks to my long time friends, Mildred Barrett and Phyllis Carman, who prayed for me during this entire project. Finally, I thank the Lord for allowing Burke and me to be a part of His plan and His book called *A Fax From Heaven*!

A note to the reader: Every effort was made to confirm and verify the authenticity of the stories you are about to read. I feel confident that all the stories in this book are genuine. Each informant provided me with an Affidavit, attesting to the fact that the information supplied was in fact the truth.

Table of Contents

Letter

Over 30 years ago I heard Elisabeth Kubler – Ross, author of the groundbreaking book, *On Death and Dying*, speak to several hundred people in Louisville, Kentucky about her studies concerning "near-death experiences" and her then recent studies on "life after death." She described herself as a "pessimistic Protestant" before her studies on death and after-death experiences. She stated that since her research, she had become convinced without a doubt, there was definitely life after death. This was a very powerful moment for me personally to hear from one who was a psychiatrist by training, make such a statement not based on faith but on scientific research.

I experienced another powerful moment several months ago when Faye Aldridge, a person whom I had never met before, entered my office at the hospital and told me a story about her husband. Two doctors who work at this hospital had seen him after his death. It was an incredible experience for them, for her and her family. This experience led her to write a book about her husband's after-death appearance and similar experiences. She feels she received a special blessing from God and so do I. She wants to share this blessing with us. This book is not research but it does contain extraordinary stories, which have come from the mouths of those who have experienced these events. I hope this book will be a source of hope and peace as you read these words and reflect on the stories. Life is a mystery but sometimes the mystery comes to us face to face to reassure us of the unknown. I applaud the work of Faye Aldridge and I hope this book will minister to those who read it.

Lewis M. Lamberth, Jr.
Director of Pastoral Services
Baptist Hospital
Nashville, Tennessee

CHAPTER 1

A Fax From Heaven

"Every once in a while, something happens to you that you just can't explain. You know, when all you can do is take pause or stand still in complete awe . . . that night between 11:30 and 12:00, as I sat alone on the couch in my family room, something happened. Initially I was frightened and uneasy, only to be overcome, just as suddenly, by a sense of peace and calmness like I have never known before. There was a translucent form there, which I did not recognize. Then I heard a voice, which I had heard before say, 'I have gone to heaven to be with God. Don't worry about me, I am okay.' I knew that voice. I didn't need to call the hospital to find out that Mr. Aldridge had gone on to be with God, just as he had said."

The preceding paragraph is an excerpt from a letter written by Dr. Carl Willis, a Nashville oncologist. Dr. Willis was stunned when a deceased patient appeared in his living room and spoke to him. Later, he learned he was not the only physician who experienced an after-death appearance from Burke Aldridge.

My husband, Burke, had been under a physician's care for months; suffering from continuous pain had become a way of life for him, but the source of the pain remained a mystery. On a cold February night in 2005, I rushed him to the emergency room at Baptist Hospital in Nashville, Tennessee. His pain had reached an unbearable level and was accompanied by acute respiratory distress.

The emergency staff responded at once when they realized the severity of Burke's symptoms. His right lung had collapsed. Within minutes, the nurse started him on oxygen and administered an injection of morphine to lessen the severe chest pain. Burke was admitted to the critical care unit, a unit reserved for only the most life-threatening conditions.

For the next five days, Burke's body was probed, biopsied, scanned, and X-rayed. The pain never decreased and his inability to breathe became nearly unbearable. It was hard to believe this critically ill man had been busy living an active life only days before. Now my strong, 53-year-old husband slipped in and out of consciousness, engaged in a battle for his life.

I did all I could to make him comfortable. He knew how much I loved him and I assured him that I would remain by his side. I prayed for him and I read Scripture to him even when he was not conscious. I knew his spirit had to remain strong in order to fight the attack against his body.

On the sixth day, the biopsy results confirmed the worst: Burke had lung cancer and it had spread to his spine. He was in the fourth and final stage with a life expectancy of only thirty days. Burke calmly listened to the ominous prognosis, then looked at me and said, "Where is the fear? It's strange but there is no fear." I understood and agreed with him because I was also free of fear. We both knew God was with us in the midst of the chaos and we were extremely grateful for His presence.

How do you tell your children you are dying? How do you find the right words?

As a father, Burke was amazing! From day one, he participated in the care of our son and daughter, David and Donna. When they were babies, he rocked them to sleep and fed them as often as I did. When they were young children, he nurtured them and played games with them. Burke always had the unique ability to see life through their eyes, never expecting them to see life through his. As the children grew, they often sang and played guitar with their dad. Our family loved, laughed, and was openly affectionate. We were happy together and it was too soon to say goodbye.

The evening after we had received the doctor's prognosis, the children arrived at the hospital. I sat near by and listened as Burke told them the dreadful news. A feeling of helplessness crushed me as I watched them attempt to control their emotions. Tears welled in their eyes and spilled over in silence as they tried to be strong for their dad. We had never experienced that kind of pain before. I could almost hear their hearts break. I felt as if a part of me was dying.

It was Burke's nature to find the good in any situation, a quality that did not fail him even in that terrible moment of realization. Gently, Burke told the children how wonderful it was to love them, to be their dad, and to have shared their life with them. He spoke plainly to them of the importance of faith in our Lord. He reminded them to look past this temporary life toward the approaching life eternal, where the word goodbye does not exist. He expressed his desire that God would use the situation and cause something good to come from his premature death.

It was late when David and Donna went home and I settled down in a chair, wanting to sleep—to escape reality. Burke's breathing was laborious. He was in excruciating pain and restless in the unfamiliar hospital bed. It was a night filled with bittersweet emotions. We all lived through that day, but I believe it was the most heartrending day we ever endured.

The following days and nights turned into a blur of continuous mental and physical anguish. Family and friends came for brief visits. They came to say goodbye to a very deserving and special person whose life appeared to be drawing to a close. Outside the door they wept, then dried their eyes before entering the room.

Burke bravely faced his last days though weary from relentless pain and the ever-present struggle to breathe. He described his intense pain as half-physical and half-heartsick pain. Leaving his loved ones caused him great distress. As others hid their tears, so did I. I hid them well in an attempt to spare him even more pain. He could not bear to think of leaving me alone, so I pretended I was a rock even when I felt like a pebble.

The morning of February 28, day twenty-two of Burke's final journey, began with a fine, cold rain. Gray clouds hovered over the city. I stood by his bed watching him sleep and listening to each breath. He was heavily sedated. For the moment, I was thankful he was not hurting.

Suddenly, his eyes opened and he smiled a radiant smile! He told me he had been with the Lord! He said the Lord had showed him things of heaven and spoke to him about them. With great peace he told me, "The Lord said I can come home and He will help me cross over." My husband reminded me that his quality of life had diminished to the point where he was no longer living, merely existing in agony. With no hesitation and an unmistakable anticipation, Burke told me he was ready to go. I could no longer hide my tears and they fell down my face. He smiled at me and said, "No regrets." My heart was breaking, but I nodded and agreed, "No regrets."

I did not give up at that time but I did give in. I accepted God's will. I knew Burke was in God's hands and His will would soon be done. My prayers changed; I no longer prayed for Burke to stay on earth. I promised him I would remain beside him and hold his hand until Jesus took his other hand to lift him up to heaven. He assured me that he would meet me there when it was my turn to cross over.

In a short time, the Lord allowed me to keep my promise; I held Burke's hand as his life on earth ended later that same day. Death came for him just before midnight. As I held Burke's hand in mine, I became aware of a holy presence! Although it was beyond my physical sight, I knew beyond doubt that an angelic presence saturated the very atmosphere of the room! There was a strong feeling of anticipation in the air as Burke's spirit left his body! If I had reached above my head, I believe I could have touched the angels! In my spirit, I could hear them rejoicing, "Burke's coming home, Burke's coming home!" I found comfort in the knowledge that his life in heaven was about to begin!

I called the children after Burke died and they came to say goodbye. We left the hospital just before three o'clock in the morning as giant, unpredicted snowflakes blanketed the streets. Snow had not been in the forecast; however, Burke had repeatedly mentioned seeing snow the day before. Against the wishes of the children, I drove home alone. I had to reconcile within my heart the reality of my situation.

My strength was gone. Exhaustion and aloneness overwhelmed me. I could barely see the road because the snowfall was so heavy. It took me almost an hour to get to our home in the country. Darkness accentuated the lonely sound of music made by wind chimes swaying in the cold, winter wind.

I drove into the garage and pressed the remote, closing the garage door. It closed partially then raised right back up. It closed successfully on the second try. I did not think it was significant until the same thing happened the next two nights when I entered the garage. Each time, it was as if someone walked into the garage behind me, triggering the safety device. I saw no one.

I slept about three hours before David came over at eight a.m. As soon as he arrived, the phones began to ring. He answered but heard only a dial tone. The ringing continued as he moved from phone to phone all through the house. The answering machine was set to answer after four rings; however, the answering machine did not respond, though it was in perfect working condition. All the phones in the house were ringing! The ringing stopping after a dozen rings.

Suddenly, I remembered that Burke said he was going to try to send me a fax when he got to heaven letting me know he was all right! I said as much to David. He bounded up the stairs to my office and discovered the fax machine was unplugged! We shook our heads in disbelief, uncertain of what just happened.

Two days later, Dr. Arthur Cushman, a neurosurgeon, and his wife, Carolyn, visited our family at the funeral home. Dr. Cushman called me aside and told me a miraculous, unusual report—Burke had appeared in his home the night before, nearly twenty-four hours after his death! He said Burke appeared to him in the center of a white light. He described what he saw: "Burke's body was surrounded by a white light like a white halo. He looked very healthy and happy and appeared to be younger than at the time of his death." Burke spoke to him saying, "Don't worry Slim, I'm alright." (Slim was a nickname Burke had called him for many years.) Dr. Cushman continued, "He then gradually faded out of sight. There was no one else with him, but I could tell he was in a beautiful land filled with flowers; I could see the flowers behind him. This is the only time I have ever had an experience like that. I sure am glad that Burke came to tell me 'goodbye'!"

My family and I welcomed this news as a rare gift from God. We knew Burke was a Christian and we believed he had gone to heaven. The news of Burke's after-death appearance to Dr. Cushman was a welcome source of encouragement. My family and I gained strength when we learned of the encounter. Amazement and appreciation filled me in response to the Lord's generous gift. I sensed that God was reminding me, "I am with you; you are never alone."

Less than two weeks later, I had a conversation with Dr. Willis, Burke's oncologist. He, too, had a story to tell. He told me Burke had visited him in his home on the very night he died! Dr. Willis reported he was in his family room reading a book that night. He saw something unusual in his peripheral vision—a shimmering white light. As he refocused his eyes, the light began to manifest into the shape of a man's body. Dr. Willis could not clearly see the man's face because the man was translucent. Dr. Willis was astounded when he heard Burke's voice say, "I have gone to heaven to be with God. Don't worry about me. I am okay."

Dr. Willis said in a letter to me, "I knew that voice. I didn't need to call the hospital to find out that Mr. Aldridge had gone on to be with God, just as he had said. He was ready for the Lord, and the Lord was ready for him, despite my intentions. I think he must have known how much I wanted to help him, and he stopped by just to let me know he was feeling a whole lot better. He was breathing a lot better and he had no more pain. He had met a better doctor who had given him rest and comfort and had granted him everlasting life. I hope this recap of my encounter brings comfort to you."

I asked both Dr. Willis and Dr. Cushman to write me a letter, documenting the encounters. Both physicians were kind enough to comply with my request. Dr. Cushman faxed a letter to me on March 29, 2005 and Dr. Willis faxed his letter to me on March 31, 2005. I was sitting at my desk reading both letters and contemplating the significance of the content when I realized the true meaning of those letters. I really did get a fax from heaven! The message that I received from Burke by way of two physicians was, "I've gone to heaven to be with God. Don't worry. I am okay!" Two witnesses confirmed the message!

CHAPTER 2

A Yellow Rose

I carried two heavy bags of groceries from the garage into the kitchen. The house was quiet. A miniature, pink rose had been placed on the counter of the island in the center of our kitchen. A small square of folded, white paper was resting behind the beautiful rose. I picked up the note and smiled as I read: "To say I love you would be enough, I know; but I'd rather say 'I love you' with a rose." The note was signed, "Love, Burke."

I placed the rose in a small vase of water, tucked the little note in my wallet between my library and voter registration cards, and then promptly forgot about the heartwarming little gift.

I absolutely love flowers and they were a recurring theme in our marriage; beginning with the beautiful gardenias that filled the church on the day of our wedding. The fragrance of the gardenia is sweet, aromatic, and unmistakable. Many times, I have placed a gardenia blossom or a rose bud on my pillow just so I could enjoy the wonderful fragrance as I drifted off to sleep.

Burke had given me flowers on many occasions during our 35-year marriage—sometimes roses, sometimes Stargazer lilies; however, he knew yellow roses were my favorite. I always thanked my husband and carried on over his lovely flower gifts. In hindsight, I never appreciated them enough.

My husband died only about six months after he gave me the sweet, little miniature rose.

In the days that followed Burke's death, flowers came pouring into the funeral home and the church; some were even delivered to our home. Words could never express the depths of my gratitude; each flower meant someone was remembering Burke and that fact deeply touched my heart. Three precious words echoed in my mind each time a floral arrangement was delivered; I suppose, as long as I live, flowers will always mean "I love you" to me.

After Burke's funeral, I took many of the

beautiful, fresh flowers to my now lonely home. All too soon, the colorful flowers withered and died. When there were no more fresh flowers in the house, I missed them a great deal.

Three weeks after I buried my husband, the florist delivered a very unique arrangement to my home. There were so many fresh flowers! The arrangement was nearly three feet high! I have never seen such a glorious, gorgeous array! The large, square, ivory-colored, metal container held a fabulous assortment of all kinds of flowers. Purple iris and yellow roses were predominant; they stood out strikingly above all the rest. I opened the envelope that accompanied the flowers to find my dear friend, Charline Wilhite, had sent them. She had purposefully waited to send her gift in memory of Burke, knowing that it would be even more special after all the others had faded and died. I positioned the arrangement in a place of honor—in the center of my long, dining table, in front of the kitchen fireplace.

Each morning I sat alone, sipping my coffee next to an empty chair and trying to adapt to my new way of life. But I only needed to look up and Charline's flowers gave me a bit of comfort. They spoke those same three words to my lonely, hurting heart: "I love you." I am quite certain Charline never realized how much her gift meant to me during those early days of brokenness. I tried to express my gratitude, but my words were never quite adequate.

As the days passed, one-by-one, the precious flowers drooped and died. Each day, I removed the dead ones, leaving the live ones in ample water. Finally, the day came when all the flowers were gone. Only the greenery remained alive, except for one yellow rose. I stopped adding water to the container, but, surprisingly, the gorgeous, perfectly formed little rose did not droop and it did not fade. After a month, I removed the rose from the greenery and laid it on the mantle beside a picture of my husband and me.

Though the rose remained on the mantle for many weeks and became dry to the touch, the color remained vibrant, its head never drooped, and the petals never withered! Thinking the little, yellow rose must have been treated with a preservative, I carried it with me and visited the florist to find what they had done to make it stay so perfect. Each employee looked at it and admired the rose, but no one had an explanation. One man, presumably the owner, said he had never seen a rose remain so perfectly preserved. He told me only God could do such a thing! He suggested I store it in a sealed glass container in order to keep it safe.

One day, I was sorting out the cards in my wallet and a folded, square piece of white paper fell out. I picked it up and unfolded it. Once again I read, "To say I love you would be enough, I know; but I'd rather say 'I love you' with a rose. Love, Burke." Could it be? He had been in heaven for months! Was the strange, little rose his way of saying "I love you"?

Almost five years have passed and the little rose remains the same—its vibrant, yellow petals are fully opened and the stem is still green.

Since Burke died, I have learned to accept the gifts and not question the Giver. I hear Him say "I love you" each time I look at the extraordinary, yellow rose that never died.

CHAPTER 3

Go Back

Barbara and Jerry Brantley were happily married. They lived in Grand Bay, Alabama with their five-year-old son. As a child in rural Mississippi, Barbara had dreamed of living near the ocean; her home so close to the Gulf of Mexico was a dream come true. Barbara enjoyed every minute of her life and had no inclination to be anywhere else.

It was the summer of 1977. Jerry and Barbara often played golf together on the weekends at a country club not far from their home. One beautiful, weekend day, the couple looked forward to a relaxing afternoon on the links. Jerry left first in his own car, with Andy, their son, in the back seat. Barbara had plans for later that day, so she followed closely in her own vehicle.

As the little caravan rounded a curve on the winding road, an oncoming car crossed into Barbara's lane. (The driver later claimed she veered into oncoming traffic because the sun obscured her view.) The large, Pontiac Bonneville hit Barbara's compact VW Rabbit head on. Having neglected to wear a seatbelt, Barbara was unrestrained; the impact threw her body across the car. With great force, her head, neck and back struck the metal strip between the front and rear passenger-side windows.

Five-year-old Andy witnessed the crash from the rear window of his dad's car. Jerry brought his car to a screeching halt and was at the scene of the accident within minutes. It was obvious Barbara had sustained major injuries; the back of her head had been laid open, from top to bottom. Jerry suspected her neck was broken and tried to stabilize her until an ambulance arrived. Little Andy was traumatized.

Singing River Hospital in Pascagoula provided emergency care. In addition to the massive head trauma, it was discover Barbara had sustained a broken collarbone and, as Jerry had feared, a fractured, cervical spine at two levels—her neck was broken in two places!

In order to stabilize Barbara's neck and, hopefully, prevent paralysis, she was attached to a traction devise designed to hold her head firmly in a stable position. The procedure required to attach the devise was frightening. A nurse shaved Barbara's head and an orthopedic surgeon drilled a hole in her skull above each ear. Metal tongs were screwed directly into her skull with a weighted cable attached. The contraption created a pulley device that held Barbara's head like a vise.

Barbara was in excruciating pain as her condition deteriorated. Her vital signs became unstable until, finally, Barbara stopped breathing. For a brief time, Barbara's injuries seemed to have taken her life.

Barbara will never forget the things she saw during her short, interval of death. She remembers she entered a distinctly round tunnel through which she traveled at jet-like speed. The tunnel was a beam of light and she became a part of the radiant stream. Her body was weightless and totally pain-free. Though she saw no one in the tunnel, she was aware of a presence traveling with her. When she reached the tunnel's end, she exited and saw her husband's deceased grandparents sitting in rocking chairs on a long porch. They were smiling at her. However, they had their hands extended, palms out and up, indicating she was to "Stop, and go back. Go back!"

Suddenly, and with an agonizing jolt, Barbara

was back in her body experiencing the excruciating pain from which she had escaped while in the beam of light.

Barbara endured the interminably-long, recovery process bravely, refusing to give up. She could not imagine leaving her young son without a mother, so she fought hard to live. A permanent halo replaced the cranial tongs. The halo was mounted onto her skull then connected to a body cast that enclosed her body from the top of her shoulders to her hips. She wore the cast and halo for the next four months while her fractured, cervical spine healed. Barbara's recovery was slow and required much patience and determination. But recover, she did.

Thirty-two years later, Barbara still enjoys life with minimal deficits, considering the nature of the injuries she endured. She still clearly recalls her journey through the beaming stream of light. Barbara no longer fears death; she had a brief preview of what waits on the other side!

CHAPTER 4

The Spirit of Comfort

Dawn Elizabeth Ellison and Chad Allen were married on May 23, 1998, at First United Methodist Church in Lexington, Mississippi.

Before the wedding, Dawn presented her mom with a letter. A portion of it read, "The most important day in my life! Finally, I am going to be someone's wife! My mother, my friend…always there to protect me with your unselfish air. You are truly my angel on earth. Thank you for giving me life. I love you more than you could ever know. Thank you, Mommy!"

Dawn's wedding day was perfect and the heartwarming ceremony was special in every way. The attractive couple fairly beamed their joy. Dawn looked radiant—a vision in glowing white! She wore a long veil and a simple-but-elegant, floor-length gown. To complete her lovely attire, she wore a brand new pair of high-top, navy, Converse All-stars! Conventional, Dawn was not!

Dawn was born on August 11, 1974; the "bonus

child" of John and Bonnie Ellison. Dawn's siblings, Gaye, Mike, and Glenda, ages 9 to 15, adored her at first sight and carried her everywhere with them. Dawn thrived with all the attention and loved her brothers and sisters dearly. She enjoyed a happy and contented childhood as she grew up in her loving, Christian home.

Dawn was a lovely girl with blond hair and sparkling, brown eyes. Always small for her age, Dawn grew to be a strong, feisty, tomboy who wanted things her own way. She was active in sports; she played hard and always played to win! Losing was failure and failure was not a concept Dawn would ever entertain!

Dawn grew into a talented athlete—first in softball; then, in high school she became a powerful, three-point shooter for her basketball team. In her senior year, Dawn's basketball team won a spot in the finals for the first time in the school's history. When the buzzer sounded on the final quarter of the last game, Dawn sat on the gym floor and cried. It was the end of a treasured chapter in her life.

Truth, honesty, and integrity shaped Dawn's character. She truly cared about others and love was simply her way of life. All through high school, Dawn and Chad, her future husband, worked at a farm supply store. The two of them were invaluable employees and together they almost ran the store. Dawn graduated from high school with honors then graduated from Holmes Community College with a 4.0 average for which she received a Massey Scholarship. The scholarship covered the entire cost of the rest of her education. When she accepted the scholarship, she signed an agreement promising to give ten percent of her earnings to help others. The agreement was binding for life!

Dawn consistently and quietly helped others whenever she could. Never seeking to receive anything in return, most of her assistance was given anonymously.

When Dawn was in college, she developed an eating disorder. She was 5' 4" and weighed only 100 pounds. She chose to seek the help of a Christian counselor. Dawn began to realize her life was out of control. She made the decision to ask Jesus into her heart as her Lord and Savior. Dawn believed this decision was the best she ever made!

May of 1998 was a life-changing year for Dawn—she received her doctorate in pharmacy and married her high school sweetheart. Her new husband, Chad Allen, was in the process of finishing his degree at Mississippi State University and Dawn had been hired as a pharmacist in Mobile, Alabama. The newly weds planned to see each other on weekends until Chad was free to move to Mobile.

On November 20, 1998, Dawn got up and went to the gym, came home, showered, and left for work. When she failed to show up at the pharmacy, the manager became concerned. Dawn's car was soon discovered just outside the pharmacy doors with the driver's door ajar.

Bonnie and John, Dawn's parents came home for lunch that day to discover a phone message from Dawn's apartment manager. Their hearts sank as they heard their daughter was missing. The Ellisons contacted Chad and the three of them packed and headed for Mobile.

It was a quiet trip. There was pain in the silence; sadness in the unspoken words. Each one of them knew something painful was just ahead; a pain so dreadful none of them could bear to talk or even think about it.

Dawn's mother, Bonnie, recalls, "We were just south of Hattiesburg, traveling on Highway 98, half way between Hattiesburg and Mobile, when I experienced something that was unexplainable! This extraordinary feeling descended on me! I felt light, happy, lifted up, and so loved! I experienced God giving me a great big hug! I felt like I had swallowed sunshine! I did not understand what just happened to me; neither could I understand the knowledge that came on the heels of that experience. I knew in my heart that Dawn was dead."

At the same time, a verse from the Bible, Romans 8:26, kept repeating in Bonnie's mind: *"Likewise the Spirit also helpeth our infirmities; for we know not what we should pray for as we ought: but the Spirit itself maketh intercession for us with groanings which cannot be uttered."*

Bonnie did not immediately tell John, her husband, what she experienced. When she told him later, John surprised her by admitting he had experienced similar feelings at the same time and the same location! John told her Dawn had actually spoken to him, saying, "Daddy, don't worry about me, I am with Pappy." (Pappy, John's deceased father, had died in 1993.)

Bonnie knew God was preparing her for what was to come. She felt numb and paralyzed emotionally, no longer able to think or pray. The situation was so gut-wrenching her brain nearly shut down. She remembers worrying that Dawn might be cold without her coat in the chilly, November air.

The Ellisons and Chad arrived in Mobile and launched a major search for Dawn. The apartment manager arranged for Dawn's photo to be aired on the 10:00 news with a request for information. There was no response. Soon, many friends and family members joined in the frantic search for Dawn. Over 10,000 fliers were printed and handed out over two counties. A long-time, family friend, Joyce Barrett, came to Mobile and manned the phones, directed traffic, and got a helicopter crew to fly over the area to search for clues.

After twenty-four hours, the police became involved, officially treating Dawn as a missing person. A Christian, police detective was assigned to Dawn's case. On the third day after Dawn's disappearance, a Sunday afternoon, the detective called the family together and said the unthinkable words, "I regret to inform you…" Tears streamed down the detective's face as he told the family that Dawn was dead. He asked the family if he could have the privilege of praying with them and for them. They all joined hands and he prayed a beautiful, powerful prayer that moved their hearts to tears.

Dawn had been abducted from her car in the store parking lot by 20-year-old William Rodgers, who had been released from Atmore Prison in June. Rodgers forcibly took Dawn to a remote area of Jackson County, Mississippi. There he assaulted her and shot her six times in the face and head. Early Sunday morning, prompted by a guilty conscious and a night of drinking, the killer shot and killed two of his neighbors, then shot a police officer who responded to the resulting, emergency call. Numerous police officers were dispatched. Rodgers walked out of the house brandishing a high-powered rifle, refusing to put it down. The police were forced to fire on Rodgers to bring a halt to the deadly situation. Rodgers died instantly.

Several months after Dawn's death, Bonnie experienced another astonishing occurrence. Bonnie remembers, "I felt it coming! There was a feeling that I was going to experience something. 'Electric,' maybe, is a good word to describe the encounter!" As the strange feelings swirled through Bonnie's heart and mind, the most thrilling, surprising, unexpected thing happened: Dawn gave her mother a hug! Bonnie still can feel the incredible sensation and tears of joy still threaten as she recalls, "It was so quick that I hardly knew she was there! All she said was 'Mommy. Mommy. Mommy!'

It has now been eleven years since Dawn's death. Bonnie says, "Losing a child is devastating; it is like ripping your heart out. When we were told that Dawn was deceased, I knew exactly what was important in this life. I know that God did not kill Dawn. We never blamed God. When evil people do evil things, innocent people are hurt. God cared for us during the ordeal. I believe that God knew our need before we did; He made Himself known to us by the extraordinary experiences to give us strength to get through the ordeal. Losing Dawn has brought some family members closer to Jesus. Not all; but, praise God, some."

CHAPTER 5

His Ways

God made the heavens, the earth, and the universe. I have no doubt that He spoke light and darkness into existence and created the sun, moon, and stars. It is easy for me to accept the awesome might and power of God with the faith of a child.

However, I suppose the ways of the Lord in the details of life will seem foreign to me for as long as I am on this side of heaven. His concern over the minutiae of life will always amaze and delight me. Why would Almighty God bother Himself with the seemingly trivial or insignificant things—little things, such as an earring?

My husband and I were preparing to leave town early one morning. The car was packed and I had just fastened the clasp on my wristwatch and put on my earrings. (I made it a practice to wear small, pearl earrings whenever traveling and leave the rest of my jewelry safely at home.) I turned to walk out of the bedroom and I heard a quiet voice say, "Go, and look in the mirror." I paused for a moment questioning why I should receive such instruction then did as the voice had directed me. I turned on the light and looked closely at myself in the mirror. Then I saw it! One earring was an ordinary pearl and the other was silver pearl.

With a smile and a bit of wonder I said, "Thank you, Lord."

Would it have mattered if I had worn miss-matched earrings? Certainly not. I would have been annoyed by the mistake but it really would not have mattered in the end. But for some reason, it mattered to the Lord.

That kind of divine intervention is puzzling to me. I am so thankful that God notices everything! I just do not know why He bothers. The fact remains that He does; and I love Him for looking after me!

I remember one summer when everyone in my family had too much going on in their lives. They were always gone from home and I ended up cutting the grass until late one evening. The house was empty and quiet when I finished working in the yard and headed in for a shower. Just as I entered the bedroom, I heard a voice say, "Kneel and pray." I received no instruction as to what I should pray, but I obeyed. I stepped toward the side of the bed and dropped to my knees. I thanked God for each family member and named off several blessings. I remained there a moment just waiting for further direction, but I heard nothing else.

As I arose from my kneeling position, I turned my head to the left and looked toward the floor. A huge spider (it looked to be three inches in diameter and growing!) scurried off the leg of my jeans and onto the carpet. I killed the spider with my shoe then carried him to his final resting place. I remember just thanking God for showing me that spider before it bit me or got under the bed! He knew my aversion to spiders, and once again, He was watching over me!

One more story!

One morning, after working in the flower bed on the side of our home, I was alone in the house and walking though the upstairs hall. A voice distinctly said, "Look out the window." I walked to the nearest window and looked out over the flowerbed. I admired the freshly cut grass and the shade provided by the two, tall hickory trees in the yard; but I was puzzled by that long, straight, black stick that was near the flower bed. I was sure I had cleaned up all the debris around the flower bed and the stick should not have been there. At that moment, the long, black stick began to crawl and slither from side to side until it ended in up in the flowerbed! It was a very long, black snake. I detest snakes and avoid them with great care. When my husband returned home, he searched until he found the snake, then he carried it off by the tail. The snake wasn't poisonous, but it *was* a creepy, disgusting snake. Once again, the Lord was watching over me!

Why would anyone ever doubt God about anything? He is all-powerful, full of love and forgiveness, and He is in charge. He keeps up with the entire universe and still manages to let me know when I am wearing miss-matched earrings and warns me about spiders and snakes. He knows the exact number of hairs on my head and knows when a sparrow (or spider) falls.

"For My thoughts are not your thoughts, neither are your ways My ways, saith the Lord. For as the heavens are higher than the earth, so are My ways higher than your ways, and My thoughts than your thoughts." (Isaiah 55:8-9)

CHAPTER 6

Realities

Bart Bell's sport was tandem racing, a cycling competition in which the contestants ride bicycles built for two. However, racing tandems are far different from the recreational cycles with which most are familiar; these tandems are not equipped with brakes and they are built for speed. Propelled by two highly trained athletes, in the final lap of tandem races these mechanical marvels can reach speeds of nearly 50 miles per hour!

Bart's preferred event was the tandem sprint, a race of a little over a mile (1.66 kilometers) held in a stadium called a velodrome. The velodrome contains a 333 meter track with banked curves. The slope at either end of the velodrome track rises at an incredible 180 degrees. During a race, each tandem cycle is manned by a pilot (or captain) who steers and sets the pace, and a co-pilot (or stoker) who works in conjunction with the pilot. The two must think and act as one during these exciting and dangerous competitions. High speeds and no brakes guarantee an interesting race and an unpredictable finish!

In 1992, Bart Bell was living in San Diego, California. He had spent years perfecting his sport, the last eight in actual tandem sprint competition. At the age of twenty-four, it appeared his dream was about to come true! Bart was now an Olympian hopeful! The final race for this Olympic World Championship finalist took place in Blaine, Minnesota. The results would determine whether Bart would go to the Olympics in Barcelona, Spain as the tandem sprint pilot or would be held in reserve as the back-up captain.

On June 28, 1992, the race took place as planned. Everything was going well; Bart and teammate Tom Brinker were burning up the track at approximately 45 miles per hour when the unthinkable happened. Bart and Tom were thrown from their cycle by a mid-sprint collision.

Bart received a broken nose and suffered a severe, closed-head injury which left him comatose for two weeks. He regained consciousness but weeks passed before Bart's cognitive ability was fully restored. More than five weeks after the accident, Bart experienced his first moment of clarity when he saw the Olympic ceremonies on television. His first thought was, "I'm supposed to be there. I must have overslept!"

His cuts and scrapes healed, but Bart suffered physical deficits caused by the head injury. He was extremely lethargic, sleeping most days for eighteen to twenty hours. The left side of his body was paralyzed and the head injuries had left him with short-term amnesia. He could remember being five years old; he could recall his phone number from when he was seven; but Bart had no memory of the crash or the days immediately surrounding it. Oddly, he felt young, like a small child. It was as though his brain had taken him to a safe place to recuperate.

During his first conscious moments, Bart was aware something unusual had happened. He felt changed; something about him was different beyond the physical injuries. Bart remembers: "I knew something. I did not know what I knew, but something was different in my soul, in my heart, in my being. I did not talk about it; I just thought about it. In the days that followed, it became clearer in my head and in my heart what actually transpired."

Slowly, Bart's memory of the events he experienced while comatose returned. They became clearer as the days progressed. Bart remembers lying with his toes pointing up, as the hands of a clock would point to twelve; however, his feet seemed to be pointing toward eleven.

"I was at the gates of heaven," Bart recalls. "Even now, I don't know what you call that place where I was, because I was not inside the gates. There was a male voice which I did not recognize that told me 'Don't look at the light'. This bright, white light was coming from behind my right shoulder. I did not look at the light."

The experience continued as he remained flat on his back looking at his toes. Soon, Bart's deceased grandmother walked up and stood near his feet. Her voice was distinct and familiar. She told him "You're not going to stay; you're going back." Then, Carl Leusenkamp, Bart's coach who had died in 1990, appeared next to Bart's grandmother and imparted the same message: "You're not going to stay; you're going back." Bart's grandmother and his coach continued to encourage him, reassuring him he would be all right.

"After their visits I had no feelings of insecurity, anxiety, or hopelessness; only positive feelings," Bart remembers. "I am not sure if they spoke words with their mouths, but I am sure they spoke with love. I do know that I heard their words distinctly in their own familiar voices."

Bart struggles to describe the feelings he experienced during this strange encounter. "It's like trying to describe a roller coaster ride. As you describe it, you can feel it. I have said many times, I do not have the words in my vocabulary to describe the awesomeness of what happened to me. I do not know those words. It is beyond my vocabulary to speak of it. All I can do is make analogies. I could feel, I could taste, I could hear, I could smell; I was using all my senses and I could feel the love. The love was alive. It was a light blue mist. There was love all around me. It was just there. I do not know where it came from or where it went. It was just there; and it was overwhelming. I was experiencing love through all my senses and I was actually breathing in love."

As Bart's consciousness returned, he was filled with a "knowing." The love he experienced remained and seemed to permeate his entire being. He felt exhilaration! He had no way of knowing if this near-death experience took place at the moment of the collision or at some point during the coma.

"I don't speak of this often," Bart explains, "but

when I do, I get the same exhilaration in my heart that I felt while I was there. My dad was the first one I talked with about what happened. I told him, 'something's different, something happened.' There is more going on than our five senses can perceive. It is around us and in us. It's not scary, but it is overwhelming!"

Bart endured a long and difficult period of recovery and rehabilitation. With courage and determination, he recovered from his injuries and walks today with a mild limp. The Lord took Bart on a heavenly journey and Bart clearly received His message. He began to understand his earthly journey was really just beginning. Bart could now face his future with a new and profound understanding!

It has been seventeen years since Bart's accident. He now owns his own successful business and lives in Colorado Springs, Colorado with his wife, Carri, and their four children. Though that fateful collision ended his Olympic dreams, God left Bart with a winning spirit in his heart and the ability to fulfill his destiny. He views his near-death experience as a gift from God to help him live his life by faith. He wakes up at five thirty each morning looking for the adventure life has to offer. Bart expectantly meets each day asking of God, "What do I do today? What's next? Where do I go from here?"

Today, when Bart stops to consider the incredible experiences he has lived, his present circumstances, and the full comprehension of the place where he will spend eternity, he responds with heartfelt enthusiasm: "I am just so blessed and thankful! It's wonderful to be alive!"

CHAPTER 7

The Voice of a Friend

Summer was Annie Scheele's favorite time of year. The Atlantic shore beckoned and Annie often took her daughter, Leila, to enjoy the golden warmth of the beach near their Rockville, Maryland home. Annie was thrilled each time she watched three-year-old Leila's eyes light up with excitement as they walked across the beautiful expanse of sparkling sand to the water's edge.

Louis, the seventeen-year-old brother of Annie's childhood friend, often joined Annie and Leila on the beach that summer. Louis and Leila had formed a grand friendship. They took long walks together, waves lapping at their feet as they searched for seashells to add to Leila's growing collection. Leila adored Louis and he seemed to enjoy his time with the little girl. He became a welcome addition to their beach outings. Louis was an all-around good kid.

Annie was sure the summer of 1977 was one she would long remember.

Several months later, the bitter winds of winter descended. One particularly cold December night, Louis left a party and sat in his car as the engine idled. Unaware of the deadly carbon monoxide fumes that seeped into the vehicle, Louis soon lost consciousness. Louis' young life was cut short; he died that frozen, winter night from accidental, carbon monoxide poisoning. His premature death was a tragic ending to a life that offered so much promise.

A short time after Louis died, Leila rode in the back seat of the car as Annie navigated heavy traffic on Piercefield Road. Annie's day had been stressful and she was not nearly as focused on driving as she should have been. With her mind on other matters, Annie was oblivious to the congested intersection just ahead of her. Suddenly, she felt a strong hand grab her shoulder and she clearly heard Louis yell, "Annie, red light!" Without hesitation, she responded to the voice; she hit the brakes, bringing the car to a sudden stop just short of the busy intersection. An inevitable accident had been avoided. Had she not stopped when she did, she and Leila could have been severely injured, maybe even killed.

Thoughts raced through Annie's mind! From

the back seat, Leila said, "Mommy, Louis is with us and he told you to stop didn't he?" It was a profound moment. Louis was certainly dead. Yet, Annie could still feel his hand as he grabbed her shoulder; she could still hear his voice as he yelled the warning that saved their lives. Louis had been with them in the car and she and Leila both heard him!

Annie cannot explain her after-death encounter with Louis; but she firmly believes no explanation is necessary. Her faith was challenged, encouraged, and strengthened by the experience; and she has gained a certain and sure peace. Annie says she is keenly aware that the body is just a shell for something much greater than this temporary life; it is the container for the eternal soul!

Though the events may be beyond rationalization, Annie remains convinced that something miraculous and incredible occurred that day on Piercefield Road!

CHAPTER 8

Foretold

Gloria Raines was only thirty-two years old when she began to have severe, incapacitating headaches. Her family physician had referred her to a neurosurgeon in Nashville, Dr. Arthur Cushman. When she arrived in his office for her first appointment, she was awake and fully coherent; however, she was very drowsy.

Dr. Cushman sent Gloria directly to the intensive care unit of Nashville Memorial Hospital. Tests were immediately performed and it was discovered Gloria had elevated intracranial pressure. Dr. Cushman started her on high doses of steroids to lower the pressure in her brain. Further studies revealed Gloria was suffering the affects of a malignant, brain tumor.

Dr. Cushman met with Gloria late that same day and gently informed her of his diagnosis. He told her he would perform the surgery to remove the cancerous growth; it was scheduled for the next day.

At first, Gloria's reaction seemed typical as she absorbed the frightening news—Gloria expressed a certainty that she would die during the surgery. Many patients facing life-threatening surgery are fearful and speak of impending death, so Dr. Cushman was not overly concerned about Gloria's prediction and offered words of comfort and encouragement. However, Gloria persisted, seemingly convinced she had foreseen the coming events that would end in her death.

On the day of her surgery, Dr. Cushman visited Gloria early during morning rounds. Gloria spoke plainly to him of the premonition she had suggested the night before, "Dr. Cushman, I know I am going to die today during the surgery."

Again, the doctor tried to assure her that her fears were normal considering the situation. But Gloria seemed strangely reconciled and at peace with the fate she predicted. She proceeded to tell the doctor precise details of what she believed would take place during the surgery: who would be present, what would be said, where Dr. Cushman would be standing, and the specific events preceding her inevitable death. Dr. Cushman tried to project a confident, reassuring attitude but he felt extremely uneasy in the face of Gloria's certainty. Gloria was convinced death awaited her inside the operating room.

Later in the day, Dr. Cushman was performing a craniotomy on another patient when he received a frantic call from the intensive care unit. The nurse quickly relayed the facts of Gloria's worsening condition, "She is unconscious. She has nearly stopped breathing. Both of her pupils are fixed and dilated."

Dr. Cushman knew Gloria's condition was critical; she was fighting for her life. Dr. Cushman realized there was no time to lose. "Give the patient mannitol, (a drug that rapidly shrinks the brain) put in a breathing tube, shave her head, and send her to the operating room, at once!"

Nurses moved quickly to prepare the adjacent operating room for an emergency craniotomy. No other neurosurgeons were available that day, leaving Dr. Cushman no choice but to stop the first surgery and operate on Gloria.

When Dr. Cushman opened Gloria's skull, he discovered she had developed a massive hemorrhage. There was nothing Dr. Cushman could do to stop the appalling loss of blood. Gloria died on the operating table within minutes of the discovery.

Dr. Cushman was seriously shaken; the series of events had occurred exactly as Gloria had predicted. Vision or premonition, call it what you like, but Gloria had somehow already observed the final moments of her life on earth; she had watched herself die. She had been one hundred percent correct in her prophecy, down to the last detail!

Dr. Cushman met with Gloria's family and candidly explained what had happened. Amazingly, the family members appeared to be at peace when they received the news. They told Dr. Cushman Gloria had forewarned them of her impending death. Though they were saddened by grief, Gloria had enabled them to prepare themselves for the inevitable.

Dazed by the events of the day, Dr. Cushman returned to the surgery that had been interrupted. The surgery ended successfully, but Dr. Cushman knew he had experienced a day he would never forget.

The fictitious name, Gloria Raines, has been used to protect the identity of Dr. Cushman's deceased patient.

CHAPTER 9

No Fear

It was the summer of 1998 and Jacqueline Elkins, a former nurse and clinic manager, was going through a very difficult time in her life. Her husband had recently walked away from her and ended their marriage, leaving Jacque feeling rejected, confused, and alone. Her faith had been severely tested and shaken by the recent deaths of her father and sister. It was all too much and Jacque's heart was bruised and broken.

May 2, 1998 was a beautiful, blue-sky day. Now on her own, Jacque decided to tackle the unfamiliar task of trimming the shrubs in her yard. She borrowed a hedge trimmer and an extension cord from her son-in-law who lived across the street. Jacque connected the extension cord to the trimmer plug and tossed the cord across her shoulder to avoid cutting it.

As she trimmed the shrub from the bottom upward, the trimmer plug and cord outlet separated slightly, allowing her gold-plated necklace chain to fall into the crack. The chain acted as a perfect conductor for the electricity. As her gold cross pendant melted and the bone-jarring currents coursed through Jacque's body, the realization hit—she was being electrocuted!

Jacque remained vertical as the electrical current caused the muscles throughout her body to convulse and her heart rhythm to falter. Her eyeballs felt like they were being wrenched from their sockets! Searing pain resulted from a rupture in her right breast where the electricity exited her body. Sounds made by passing cars, the lawn mower next door, and the laughter of children down the street remained constant—her senses remained intact.

Suddenly, Jacque realized, "I am about to meet God!" At that point, she was filled with an overwhelming sense of peace. The following account is in Jacque's own words.

"I cannot describe the peace that I felt. All fear left me; I had no regrets or anxious thoughts. There was only peace. I looked up into that lovely, blue sky and I saw one billowy, cumulous-looking cloud. The distance between the cloud and me was closing in. I could not tell if the cloud was descending toward me or if I was ascending toward the cloud! The cloud was dimensional. The part of the cloud that extended closest to me was the purest white I had ever seen. Shades of dark blue, unlike the blue-sky background, rimmed the cloud and resembled a transparent, blue mist. Knowledge was imparted to me, allowing me to comprehend that Jesus was in the cloud coming for me. I was dying and Jesus gave me the intellectual capacity to know that. I was not afraid."

The thought, "Jesus, remove this cord from me," passed through Jacque's brain. Before the thought was completed, the cord fell from Jacque's body! She immediately fell to the ground, engulfed in a personal inferno. Jacque was on fire! She experienced agonizing torture as the skin on her neck and torso were swallowed by the flames.

When she was finally able to make a sound, Jacque screamed. Her son-in-law, Jim, heard and ran to her aid. The sight that met his eyes was horrific; the flames were leaping high above Jacque's head! Putting himself in danger, Jim managed to pull the burning shirt away from her severely burned body.

Jacque remained conscious as the ambulance sped toward the burn center at Vanderbilt Medical Center in Nashville, Tennessee. Though racked by intense pain, she told the doctor in the emergency room about the cloud she saw as she looked up at the sky. The doctor responded by saying, "When you are being electrocuted, you have no voluntary muscle control. It would have been impossible for you to tilt your head back to look up. You were seeing up through your spirit's eyes. You were at the point of death."

Jacque's heart began to be changed. In the midst of the emergency room chaos, Jacque became keenly aware she no longer feared death. She realized the grief she felt over the deaths of her father and sister had been miraculously replaced by a sense of knowing they were all right. Jacque knew, beyond a shadow of doubt, she had been in the presence of Jesus and had been changed by her near-death experience. It seemed all the scriptures she had ever read came to life within her. The words of Second Corinthians 5:8 echoed in her head and reverberated in her heart. *"We are confident, I say, and willing rather to be absent from the body, and to be present with the Lord."*

The intensive care unit became Jacque's home for the next three days as her condition was stabilized. Morphine dulled her pain; however, she remained cognizant of her situation and everything that was going on around her.

Jacque remembers, "I never felt alone. A huge man, who appeared to be eight feet tall, sat in a chair at the side of my bed. His shoulders, arms, and hands were large and muscular. The man's medium-length, brown, wavy hair touched his shoulders. He was dressed in khaki-colored clothing. He never looked at me. He watched the door intently. I innately knew he was a protector—an angel sent by God to keep Satan from entering my room. I knew Satan wanted me dead but God wanted me alive." No one who visited Jackie was able to see the angel, but Jacque observed him for the entire three days of her stay in intensive care.

"The thief cometh not, but for to steal, and to kill, and to destroy: I have come that they might have life, and that they might have it more abundantly." (John 10:10) The truth of this scripture was firmly embedded in Jacque's heart and mind.

Jacque's initial treatment resulted in a hospital stay of several weeks. During this time, Jacque endured numerous skin grafts and suffered from complications caused by scar tissue.

Even after her release, she was plagued by residual problems. As the damaged nerves began to regenerate, Jacque suffered relentless, intolerable pain. A build-up of fibrous, inflexible, scar tissue resulted in Jacque's inability to turn her head from side to side. Physicians were unable to alleviate the life-altering conditions with which Jacque was forced to live each day. The pain was ruthless and her suffering, constant.

On two separate occasions, Jacque attended church healing services. Two different ministers laid hands on her and prayed for healing. The changes in Jacque's condition were immediately evident as her excruciating pain subsided, and the scar tissue became more pliant, allowing her to turn her head. God's miraculous, healing power amazed Jackie!

Over the following decade, Jacque endured a hip replacement and was diagnosed with Chronic Obstructive Pulmonary Disease (COPD). Jacque also developed a pancreatic cyst. The cyst resulted in Jacque's inability to produce insulin, a condition that required three, daily injections of insulin to stabilize her fluctuating blood sugar level.

Jacque's symptoms became intense by late August of 2009. On September 9, Jacque arrived at her doctor's office with nausea, a temperature above 100°, elevated pulse, a blood sugar level of 243, elevated blood pressure, shortness of breath and chest pain. The results of the EKG were suspicious and a heart attack in progress was suspected.

An ambulance was called and arrived barely ten minutes later. The emergency medical technician began obtaining vital signs and started an IV in an effort to stabilize Jacque for transport. Oddly, he discovered a normal blood pressure, normal pulse, normal temperature, normal blood sugar of 90, and a normal EKG. The findings were favorable but puzzling; Jacque's life-threatening condition had totally disappeared in the space of a mere ten minutes! The decision was made to transport Jackie to the emergency room at Baptist Hospital in Nashville in spite of her current, total lack of symptoms.

A CT scan of Jacque's abdomen was performed. To everyone's amazement, Jacque's chronic pancreatic cyst had vanished!

Although Jacque no longer suffered from the heart attack symptoms, Tina Reeder, an EKG tech at Baptist Hospital, ran an EKG on her while she was in the emergency room. When she saw the scars on Jacque's neck and chest, she questioned Jacque as to their source. Jacque shared with her the details of her accidental electrocution and near-death experience.

The emergency room physician examined Jacque and admitted her to the hospital for observation. The next day, Tina called her and said, "You're not going to believe this! When I returned to my department after your EKG, an email was waiting for me. An author who is writing a book about miracles has asked for stories to be submitted. I would like to give you the contact information so you can share your story."

Jacque was released from the hospital the next day with instructions to decrease her insulin injections to only one at bedtime; her blood sugar level had remained normal during her confinement. Within thirty days, she stopped the bedtime insulin injection!

Jacque left the hospital convinced that the acute, heart attack symptoms had occurred and then disappeared only to put her in contact with the writer. Since the accident and near-death experience, Jacque had wanted to tell her story. She had prayed for over ten years, asking God "What do You want me to do with this? Why did You spare my life? What is my purpose?" In answer, the Lord said, "Tell them." It was then she understood why the great angel had protected her. She knew she was supposed to share what God had done for her and share her message of hope with others! Jacque strongly believes divine intervention was responsible for the unusual, miraculous series of events that saved and renewed her life!

CHAPTER 10

Perfect Timing

When I awoke, the red, digital numbers on the face of the clock glowed in the darkness; I distinctly recall the time read 4:44. As was my practice, I remained in bed and began to pray through the early morning hours. The second time I looked at the clock the time was 5:30. At that particular time, I had begun praying for my daughter who was going through a flare up of Sarcoidosis, a painful, inflammatory disease that affects all major organs, including the eyes.

As I prayed, I thought of a conversation two years earlier with a woman who also suffered from Sarcoidosis. She had done extensive research on this rare disease and had learned much about available medical treatment. Most doctors have little experience treating Sarcoidosis victims and this woman possessed a wealth of potentially beneficial knowledge. I wanted to ask her some questions. I remembered her name was Kathy, but I could not remember her last name.

I had spoken to Kathy by phone but I had never met her in person. I could not even remember who put me in contact with her in the first place; I had no way of finding her. I told the Lord of my desire to speak to Kathy and prayed, "Lord, if You want me to talk to her, You will have to have her call me."

Later that morning, I went to my daughter's home to take care of my young grandson. I answered the phone when it rang at 1:30 that afternoon. A female voice said, "This is Kathy and I'm trying to reach Faye." The woman I had prayed to find only eight hours earlier had called my daughter's home to find me! Shocked that my prayer had been answered so quickly, I asked her why she called and how she had gotten my daughter's number. She said she had been compelled to call me from the time she got out of bed that morning. Though not sure how to find me, she had remembered the woman who put us in touch initially and had given her a call. The woman had given Kathy a phone number, not realizing it was actually my daughter's. Kathy dialed the number and, lo and behold, I answered the phone at my daughter's house.

Kathy felt certain she was supposed to share the name of an ophthalmic solution with me. Since it had decreased her eye symptoms significantly, she thought it might be beneficial to my daughter. I told her about my prayer and we were both amazed at how God works! He really does hear every prayer! Some answers come swiftly and others take time, but He hears every prayer!

At 5:30 that morning, while I was speaking to God, God was speaking to Kathy. He knew exactly where I would be at 1:30 so He provided Kathy with the number she needed to reach me at that precise time. God had answered my prayer, even as I prayed!

God's ways are wonderful! Sometimes, I think He works in such ways to cause me to pause, look up, and ask, "What, Lord?" I can almost hear Him respond, "Did you get that? Do you think there is anything I cannot handle? Do you realize I know your every thought, your every word, and your every prayer, even before it is prayed?"

God does work in mysterious ways and I am thankful He is always attentive to my every need!

CHAPTER 11

Can You See Me?

Courtney Bordelon lived with her doting parents, Gloria and James, in Sallis, Mississippi. It was a small, quaint town located approximately fifteen miles from the historic Natchez Trace.

Courtney was no ordinary child; she was born an "old soul". While her friends watched cartoons, she avoided animated shows, preferring real people and real things. Courtney was shy and reluctant to carry on a conversation with strangers, but was open and affectionate with the people she loved. She was intelligent, witty, and usually the center of attention.

One day, Gloria was preparing to drive to the movie store in a nearby town. Four-year-old Courtney demanded she be able to dress herself for the trip. Rather than argue with the opinionated child, Gloria complied. Soon, Courtney came prancing from her room wearing mismatched colors, stripes, and polka dots, topping off the outlandish outfit with a huge bow on top of her head. With no further conversation, mother and daughter got in the car and began their short drive.

As they drove along Courtney asked, "Mamma, how do I look?" Without looking at her daughter, Gloria assured her she looked fine. The highly-offended child replied, "You haven't even looked at me!" Gloria reminded her outspoken little girl that she could not drive and look at her at the same time. Courtney did not miss a beat before she declared, "You don't know what it's like to be seventeen years old and trapped in a four-year-old body!" It was a hilarious moment, but that statement portrayed the real Courtney!

As she grew, Courtney remained a vivacious, precocious child. No one would have guessed she had been born with a genetic, liver disease. Throughout her young life, she dealt with her disease with a courage and maturity that belied her years.

By the time she turned fifteen, Courtney had become a beautiful, young woman with shoulder-length, sandy-colored hair, dark complexion, and big, brown eyes. However, it was obvious living with the chronic illness had taken a toll on her. The disease had progressed alarmingly; the only thing that could save the young teenager's life was a liver transplant.

An acceptable donor was found and Courtney received the life-saving operation. Hope flickered in the hearts of her loving parents. Their hope was short-lived when only a short time after the surgery, Courtney developed life-threatening complications. Courtney Bordelon died on the 24th day of September, 1998 — her mother's birthday.

Losing Courtney was devastating for her family. They loved her so much! Giving her up was the hardest thing they had ever had to do. Gloria felt as if a part of her body had been cut away; the pain deepened with each passing day.

About two weeks after the funeral, Gloria was awakened one night by someone shaking her leg and calling to her. She opened her eyes, sat up in bed, and was startled to find Courtney sitting on the foot of her bed, legs dangling over the side and swinging back and forth, as she had done many times before!

Gloria exclaimed, "Oh, I've been so worried about you!"

"Don't Mamma; I am fine. I am fine!" Courtney replied.

"Well, I can't believe you are here! Can you see me?" Gloria asked.

Courtney rolled her brown eyes at her mom and said, "Yes, I can see you; you can see me, can't you?"

Gloria smiled and said, "Yes, I can!"

Then Courtney replied sweetly and sincerely, "I didn't want you to worry."

Gloria told her daughter she loved her and Courtney responded with four, precious words, "I love you, too." Courtney then faded from sight!

Gloria was stunned by the encounter, but comforted and filled with a calm, sure peace. She had proof that Courtney was alive and well, just living in another place! Gloria knew she would see her daughter again in the future.

The certainty of being reunited with Courtney has given Gloria the strength to endure the heartache; and the memory of Courtney's after-death visit continues to fill her heart with hope and encouragement. Gloria's heart is now filled with the assurance that Courtney's spirit lives on in a better place; she has proof in the form of a miracle from God!

CHAPTER 12

Hope for Tomorrow

Harold and Beverly Sutton were blessed with a picture-perfect life. The happily married couple had three wonderful children: Wayne, a college sophomore, Ricky a high school senior, and Ramona, their adored little sister. The Suttons were Christians; caring and giving people who were active in their church and community. Harold was a successful realtor and land developer in a booming real estate market. It seemed the Suttons had realized all their hopes and dreams for a contented, successful life.

Harold and Beverly were proud of their little family. Wayne and Ricky were fine young men, full of love and laughter. Their youngest child, Ramona, completed their little family perfectly. The five Suttons shared a wonderful life and enjoyed every minute together. Each day was an adventure lived with anticipation, enthusiasm, and appreciation.

Life was good for the Sutton clan; but life turns

on a dime.

Life as the Sutton family knew it ended abruptly one horrible night. They received the devastating news that Wayne and Ricky had suffered a fatal automobile collision; both their fine, young sons were gone. Death came suddenly; there was no time to say "good-bye."

Harold, Beverly, and Ramona had strong faith, yet they wondered how they could endure their tragic loss. The family came to understand the death of a child is one of the worst tragedies a human can bear.

In spite of their pain, the world kept turning and days turned into years. Life went on; but, for Harold, the grief remained unbearable. One morning he went to the cemetery and stood at the foot of the graves. His broken heart was filled with an unrelenting sense of loss that had only grown more agonizing over the two years since the death of his sons. In tears, Harold spoke to the Lord. He acknowledged his sons were safe; he was certain they were in heaven enjoying more than he could ever have given them on earth. But this father's heart could not find comfort. Harold cried out to God, "Lord, can you help me with this pain? It's just more than I can stand!"

There was no audible reply to his cry; however, the crushing sorrow diminished instantly. Harold still experienced the pain of separation, but it was suddenly bearable. Harold was amazed!

He remembered a picture of a man walking along the seashore. Two sets of footsteps could be seen, imprinted in the sand along the path the man had walked. The story behind the picture suggests that Jesus always walks beside us although we cannot see Him. At critical times in our lives, only one set of footprints can be seen. Those are the times when Jesus picks us up and carries us in his arms because He knows we cannot go on in our own strength. Harold felt as though the picture had become a reality; Jesus, knowing Harold could not go on alone, had lifted him up and held him close.

Shortly after Harold's grave-side encounter, Beverly's uncle suffered a heart attack and died. Emergency measures restored him to life. He was angry when he came back from his near-death experience, exclaiming he had not wanted to return! "If you could only see what I saw, you would understand! The beauty of the sights and colors in heaven were so extraordinary! The divine music was unimaginable and incomprehensible! I just didn't want to leave it," he declared. He gave explicit instructions for the next time he died—no one was to bring him back! His family gave him full assurance that his instructions would be followed.

About one year later, Beverly was awakened one night by the sound of Harold crying in his sleep. Assuming he was dreaming of their deceased sons, she gently woke him. But Harold's dream was not filled with the grief of death; it was an encounter with life after death!

Harold dreamed of being in a strange building, resembling a duplex. He stood in a doorway of the structure, watching his son, Wayne, as he approached. Wayne appeared to come over a lush, grassy hill, walking toward Harold who was delighted to see his son's smiling face. When Wayne reached the building, he turned and entered an alternate door. When he reappeared, he carried something in his arms, but Harold could not see what it was. Wayne retraced his steps and walked back across the grassy slope. He repeatedly looked back over his shoulder at his dad. Just before he disappeared from sight, Wayne stopped, looked back with a smile on his face, and waved to his dad! Harold asked him to come back for just a minute; he wanted to hear his son's voice and look into his eyes. Harold's tears had been caused by his son's silent refusal to stop and talk with him.

Ten minutes after the dream, Harold and Beverly received a phone call. They learned that Beverly's uncle had just died and, this time, no one attempted to resuscitate him. Apparently, the death and the dream happened at the same time! Harold felt relieved; he was convinced Wayne had been sent to escort his uncle beyond death's door. Could it be Wayne now serves God by guiding people to heaven?

Several months later, Harold attended a Chamber of Commerce meeting where an evening meal was served. While at the dinner, he developed severe abdominal, chest, and arm pain. Suspecting a heart attack in progress, friends rushed Harold to the fire hall in the small town of Mt. Juliet, Tennessee and an ambulance was called.

It was almost seven o'clock in the evening but much daylight remained and the area was well illuminated. As they awaited the ambulance, Harold sat outside the fire hall in excruciating pain and struggled to breathe. His symptoms continued to worsen and Harold realized he could be dying. He tried to fight the panic that arose by focusing on his surroundings. As he looked upward toward the roof of the fire hall, his sons appeared!

Wayne and Ricky were sitting on the roof of the fire hall with their legs dangling over the edge, in the way one would sit on the tailgate of a pickup truck. They were dressed in white shirts, black tuxedos, black bowties, and black shoes, as if they were about to attend a formal gathering. They did not speak; they smiled continuously at their dad as their legs swung back and forth. Harold was overcome by a feeling of comfort and peace; he began to relax. Harold thought, "If I die, I'll go and be with the boys and if I live, I will stay here with Beverly and Ramona; in either case, I'll be okay!" He began to breathe easier and his pain diminished. Wayne and Ricky disappeared as suddenly as they had appeared. To Harold's mind, the extraordinary occurrence had seemed somehow normal and natural.

The ambulance arrived and Harold was taken to a nearby hospital. He was treated and, after a few days, underwent a successful, heart bypass surgery.

The heart surgeon talked with Harold about the visit from his sons occurring at that crucial time. The surgeon explained that Harold's ability to relax during the heart attack had allowed much-needed oxygen and blood to circulate more freely. He concluded by saying, "I believe your sons saved your life".

Harold now looks back over all the fantastic events he experienced: God had comforted his heart and made the unbearable, bearable; the reality and grandeur of heaven had been revealed; and the continued, vibrant life of his departed sons had been seen by his own eyes. Harold believes these events were God's merciful way of saying, "Everything is okay. Continue to live your life to the fullest and to the very best of your ability. One day, you will have My promise: you and your loved ones will be reunited and will be together for all time."

CHAPTER 13

A Message of Hope

Laura had grown up in the Church of Christ. She knew about Jesus and had often heard the message of salvation. But Laura spent most of her life running from God, refusing to accept His free gift of new, abundant life through His Son.

Determined to live her life according to her own rules, Laura ran, head-long, into a lifestyle of self-destruction. She became a drug user and ultimately, a drug addict. When her funds were exhausted, Laura became a prostitute to fund her habit. Tomorrow was never on Laura's radar; she spent her days in the effort to feed her growing addiction.

Circumstances intervened in Laura's wasted life when she learned she was dying of cancer. Impending death cast a shocking clarity to her shattered life and meaningless existence. Laura was filled with shame and regret. She began to realize her need of God. Laura's bruised and hardened heart became more tender and open;

she was ready to accept God's salvation—she was ready to follow Jesus.

Laura was admitted to Baptist hospital for treatment to prolong her life. Chaplain Lewis Lamberth visited her often during her stay. He spent time getting to know her and telling her about Jesus. He explained to her how Jesus died on the cross for each of us so our sins might be forgiven; he told her the blood of Jesus covers all sin. Understanding began to dawn on Laura; God's truth became a beacon of hope. Finally, Laura prayed a simple, but heartfelt prayer. She asked God for forgiveness and accepted Jesus as her Savior and Lord.

Once Laura had committed her life to Jesus, she wanted to do all her newly-found Lord required. Having never been baptized, Laura felt a strong need to do so. She wanted to make a statement about her decision to follow the Lord and to confirm her new life in God. Chaplain Lamberth was more than thrilled to comply with her wishes. Although Laura had grown up in the Church of Christ, she elected to be baptized by the pouring of water instead of being immersed.

Soon after her baptism, Laura left the hospital with a new hope in spite of her dire prognosis. She lived for only a few more months before returning to Baptist Hospital to die.

After Laura's death, her sister-in-law contacted Chaplain Lamberth and told him an interesting story. She and her husband were lying in bed asleep on the night of Laura's death. It was ten o'clock in the evening when she awoke to see Laura standing near the foot of the bed. She looked twenty years younger than her actual age and she was dressed in white clothing. Laura said, "I'm okay, don't worry!" She said nothing further before she faded out of sight! Laura's sister-in-law immediately phoned the hospital. The nurse informed her that Laura had died only minutes before.

Laura's sister-in-law knew Chaplain Lamberth had been instrumental in Laura's conversion. She believed Laura wanted him to know that she had indeed made it to the other side and was in heaven, doing just fine!

Chaplain Lewis Lamberth, Jr. is still about doing God's work. Today, he is the Director of Pastoral Care at Baptist Hospital in Nashville, Tennessee.

A fictitious name was used to protect the identity of the deceased.

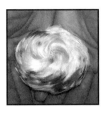

CHAPTER 14

Crown of Life

The Pitchford family of Patton, Missouri became complete when Mary was born. Sadie, her loving mother, adored the tiny infant. Her desire to protect her daughter blossomed full-grown the moment she held the baby in her arms. With great care, she gently placed Mary on a soft, feather pillow for her first contented nap.

Mary grew into a vibrant toddler, bringing joy and laughter into the Pitchford home. All too soon, Mary outgrew her little pillow bed; but she fell asleep each night with her tiny head nestled into its comforting folds.

In the winter of 1911, two year old Mary fell extremely ill. Although Sadie diligently tended her frail daughter, her constant love and care were not enough to save little Mary's life. On the tenth day of December, Mary's vibrant spirit left her body. Her precious little head rested for the final time on the little feather-pillow bed.

The joyous season of Christmas was at hand, but it was grief, not joy, that filled the Pitchford home. The memory of Mary's sweet, little voice seemed to echo in the empty house like a sad, love song, ending with "good-bye".

In the days that followed Mary's death, Sadie became emotionally attached to that little, feather pillow. She often found herself holding it closely in an attempt to fill empty arms that felt useless and awkward in the absence of her child.

One day, as Sadie caressed the pillow, she noticed a lump inside that had never been there before. She had fashioned the pillow herself; she knew it contained only an abundance of soft feathers. Quickly, Sadie cut the pillow open and was amazed to discover a strange, artistically-formed object. Hidden deep within the pillow was a flawless, extremely beautiful, white, feather crown! The little crown was about four inches in diameter and two inches tall; it would have fit Mary's head perfectly.

The Pitchford family had no explanation for

the extraordinary work of art. They accepted it with an attitude of faith, believing it to be a gift from God. To them it symbolized the crown of life little Mary had received from God's loving hands. The little crown became a reminder that Mary was in God's perfect care for all time and the cloud of grief became easier to bear. As the years passed, amazement and gratitude replaced the sadness in their hearts!

The little feather crown is now in the possession of Sadie's great-grandson, Bruce Watkins, of Hendersonville, Tennessee. The ninety-eight-year-old gift of hope remains in impeccable condition and is revered by the Watkins family!

CHAPTER 15

A Servant's Heart

A sense of freedom, security, and purpose stirred in Jaimee Underwood as she traveled toward Knoxville, just east of Nashville, Tennessee on Interstate 40. She was a single mother of two small children and a successful criminal defense attorney living in Franklin, Tennessee. Jaimee was a strong-willed woman who had recently survived a painful divorce and the premature death of her father whom she dearly loved. She had gone through some tough emotional times but with much determination, she was getting her life back on track.

Instinctively, Jaimee focused on the positive, looking forward to a great weekend. Her thoughts drifted toward the anticipated reunion with her six-year-old daughter, Alexa, and her two-year-old son, Lawson; they had spent a week with their dad and Jaimee was anxious to see them.

Jaimee was driving in the far left lane of four eastbound lanes of traffic when she ran over a small object that punctured her tire, causing it to go flat immediately. She pulled the huge SUV to the left shoulder of the road into an extremely narrow space between the heavy, speeding traffic and a large, concrete barrier. The flat tire was on the passenger's side, nearest the oncoming traffic. Jaimee realized the danger of her situation. She reported her predicament to her motor club and the Tennessee Highway Patrol was contacted for assistance.

Police Officer, Christy Dedman, responded to the call. She pulled her patrol car close behind Jaimee's vehicle and activated the emergency lights of the cruiser. Everything was by-the-book — the scene was a textbook example of safe procedure employed in an effort to divert traffic around the disabled SUV long enough for Jaimee to change the tire.

Jaimee remembers looking into the smiling face of Officer Christy Dedman as they both tried to laugh about their precarious dilemma. Seconds later, Jaimee found herself lying on the ground, dazed, confused, in excruciating pain. An eastbound tractor-trailer rig, traveling at 70 miles per hour, had crashed into the back of the patrol car, which in turn, crashed into Jaimee and Officer Dedman.

Jaimee was pinned beneath a 250-pound piece of the demolished police car. Her breathing was limited and the pain was indescribable. An off-duty paramedic emerged from one of the vehicles caught in the standstill traffic that now backed up for several miles due to the horrific accident. Jaimee feared she was dying but the paramedic assured her she would be fine; the look on his face said otherwise. Jaimee began to pray that she would live long enough to say good-bye to her children and family. The paramedic stayed with Jaimee until help arrived, holding her head so she could not see the body of Christy Dedman lying motionless beside her. Christy had died instantly.

An ambulance rushed Jaimee to the trauma center at Vanderbilt Medical Center in Nashville. She was critically injured and losing blood at an alarming rate; however, she remained awake and aware during the entire ordeal, resisting the ever-present urge to allow her mind to be overtaken by darkness and oblivion. Jaimee had sustained a traumatic brain injury, lacerations to her spleen, liver, and kidney, and an "open book" pelvic fracture that left her pelvic bone shattered into three pieces. The internal bleeding was profuse, requiring numerous blood transfusions. Jaimee's pelvic fracture necessitated surgery. Her pelvic bones were restructured with large screws and metal rods; they literally held her together. After suffering two collapsed lungs, Jaimee's condition was finally stabilized.

One of Jaimee's nurses was exceptionally kind and considerate; she went above and beyond the call of duty to be helpful. One morning shortly after the accident, the nurse shared an extraordinary account with Jaimee. "When I was with you in your room last night, I felt Christy Dedman's presence very strongly. I had finished cleaning you up and I went to the sink to wash my hands. When I looked in the mirror, I saw Officer Christy Dedman behind me. She was standing there in her uniform and hat, just smiling." The nurse told Jaimee that when she turned from the mirror, Christy was no longer there.

Morphine was administered to control Jaimee's relentless pain, leaving her thinking somewhat impaired. To make matters worse, Jaimee was suffering from survivors' guilt; she was emotionally devastated. She could not understand why her life was spared and not Christy's. Perhaps Jaimee's altered mental state is the reason Christy appeared to the nurse instead of Jaimee.

Jaimee's nurse reported seeing Officer Dedman in Jaimee's room on several occasions over the next few days. Christy always appeared in uniform, standing there smiling! Each time, Christy vanished when the nurse turned to look at her. It seemed Christy wanted to be assured Jaimee was okay and to let her know she was also fine. Jaimee immediately shared the details of Christy's after-death appearance with her best friend, JL Puckett, who came from St. Augustine, Florida, to assist her during her recovery. Jaimee and JL believed this was God's merciful way of saying, "Christy is fine, don't worry."

Jaimee underwent six surgeries over the next two years and her weight dropped below a hundred pounds. She learned to walk again in the Stallworth Rehabilitation Center at Vanderbilt Medical Center. While she was recovering, Jaimee recalls crying and declaring, "Thank You God! No matter how bad it gets, I still have one more day with my children, with my family. I have one more day to do whatever You want me to do." The traumatic experience allowed her to regain her faith in people, but more importantly, her faith in God was renewed!

Starting over again in the work place was not

easy after sustaining a brain injury. Jaimee was not the same person she was before the accident. Attorneys Alan Poindexter and Jere McCulloch encouraged Jaimee and believed in her, giving her no choice except to believe in herself. Their support and encouragement bolstered her confidence as she struggled to resume her career. Jaimee was thankful for the second chance and seized the opportunity. She began incorporating the strong sense of compassion, understanding, and patience she had acquired from her ordeal into her daily interactions with clients and colleagues.

July 19, 2009 marked five years since the date of the accident. Jaimee has recovered and now practices law with the firm of Rochelle, McCulloch, and Aulds in Lebanon, Tennessee. Through all the adversity, she learned to look for the good in people. She remembers Christy's kind spirit, her sweet smile, and her eagerness to protect and serve even in the face of peril. Instead of living life filled with survivor's guilt, Jaimee now lives with a heart filled with gratitude for an incredible gift from God. Christy's after-death appearance spoke clearly to all concerned; though her body had died, she had not ceased to exist; she was and is safely on the other side!

Jaimee will never forget the paramedic who comforted her or those special nurses who went beyond the call of duty to care for her. The family, friends, neighbors, and strangers who helped in so many ways will stay in her memory. Jaimee still keeps a large box of cards and letters containing heart felt messages of faith, hope, and love; many of them are from total strangers. Jaimee earnestly declares, "The experience was a powerful thing that changed my life."

Officer Christy Dedman died at the age of thirty-five, leaving behind a loving family: her parents, a brother, aunts, uncles and cousins. Christy was assigned to the Hermitage precinct when she was killed on July 19, 2004. She was the second female Nashville police officer to have been killed in the line of duty. Officer Dedman was posthumously awarded the highest honor bestowed by the Nashville Police Department —the Medal of Valor. Today a simple cross on Interstate 40, just east of Nashville, marks the place where Christy's life in this world came to a tragic end.

CHAPTER 16

Divine Journey

As he did everyday, Alvin Glenwood Watkins (Glen) climbed aboard the long, yellow school bus and began his assigned route through the streets of Farmington, Missouri. A veteran bus driver, Glen was cautious and he drove the huge vehicle with care; always aware he carried precious cargo. Glen never failed to consider the well-being of the children as he picked them up and took them home each day.

This day had begun like any other normal day. As he expertly maneuvered the bus filled with sixty-six children, Glen was unaware that he had embarked upon a totally unexpected, divine journey.

All was routine and the bus traveled uneventfully along when, without warning, Glen experienced a terrible, crushing pain in his chest. He pulled the bus to the side of the road and engaged the emergency brake before he collapsed and fell across the steering wheel. Glen had suffered a massive heart attack. A student ran to the nearest building and called for help.

Glen's body remained inside the bus but his spirit took flight to another land. As realization dawned, Glen found himself standing before an awesome, arched gateway! The breathtaking structure marked the entrance to a land of beauty beyond words. As he looked through the gateway, Glen saw an unending field of brilliantly-colored flowers stretching out in all directions! The colors were vivid, rich, and indescribable! Each flower was unique, perfect, and superior to anything he had ever seen on earth! Glen experienced an extraordinary perceptive ability; he knew, without being told, he could not go beyond the gates. Somehow, he was acutely aware it was not his time; he was compelled to return to his life on earth.

Glen survived the heart attack; though his body had been seriously weakened, he slowly recovered. He later told his son, Bruce, about his near-death experience. Glen was absolutely certain he had died and arrived at the gates to heaven!

The beauty Glen saw, the peace he felt, and the joy that filled his soul became memories so precious, so personal, and so cherished that he could barely speak of his experience. With tears streaming down his face, Glen said, "Human words seem to degrade the holiness of the experience." Glen found it impossible to adequately convey what he had experienced; the story of his divine journey was rarely told. Glen stored the memories within his heart and cherished them for the rest of his life.

Over thirty years later, Glen suffered another heart attack and passed from this world. Glen's son, Bruce Watkins, recalls the strange mixture of emotion he experienced during his father's funeral. The separation from his dad was heart-rending, but Bruce had such an overwhelming peace and assurance about his father's destination that he found tears seemed somehow unwarranted. Just before Glen's casket was closed, Bruce looked at his dad one last time and said, "Dad I hate to see you go." Still, there were no tears. Bruce could almost hear his dad reply, "Don't cry for me son. I'm fine!"

Bruce is convinced, beyond a shadow of doubt, his father has now crossed through that breathtaking archway. Glen has experienced the inestimable joy of entering heaven through those marvelous gates! One can only imagine the joy Glen experiences each day as he kneels at the feet of Jesus, the One who died on the cross. Enveloped in the unspeakable peace and love of that holy place, Glen has now begun a new life—a divine journey in the kingdom of God.

.

CHAPTER 17

A Very Good Thing

Some people just stand out in a crowd; fifteen-year-old Scott Rule was undoubtedly unforgettable. With blonde hair, blue eyes, and freckles, he had an endearing face that was often lit by an easy smile. Scott was extremely popular among his friends. Everyone loved this lively teenager who lived life to its fullest.

Scott lived in Laramie, Wyoming with his parents, Dan and JoAnn Rule. His older sister, Jennifer, also lived and worked in Laramie while attending the University of Wyoming as a full-time student.

On July 7, 2001, Scott and his parents set off on a short trip to the Wyoming State Fair in nearby Douglas, Wyoming. Rather than ride in his parent's car, Scott decided to accompany his friends on the drive to Douglas. Scott was riding in the back seat of the small car when it entered an intersection and was broadsided by a pickup truck. Scott was severely injured by the massive impact.

Jennifer was at work when her mother called with the horrifying report. Her brother was in critical condition in the Douglas hospital; he was fighting for his life. Jennifer immediately left for Douglas.

When Jennifer arrived at the hospital, she learned Scott had been taken by helicopter to the state's only level-one, trauma unit, located in Casper, Wyoming. Her father's broken heart was obvious as he gave Jennifer the devastating news: Scott never arrived; he died during the flight. Jennifer's voice echoed against the hard, cold hospital walls as she screamed, "He's too young! He's too young!" Angry tears filled her eyes as pain and loss pierced her heart.

Scott's body was returned to the Douglas hospital and the family stood around his lifeless form. Jennifer's heart was further wounded as she watched her mother gently shake Scott's feet and plead with desperation, "Scottie, wake up! Please, wake up!" Jennifer was overcome by sorrow; the shock and pain had left her nearly unable to breathe.

After her parents left the room, Jennifer was alone with her little brother's body. He was lying on a gurney; he looked so different. Jennifer spoke to Scott in a way only a big sister can: "Scott, I need you to be with me. I need you to help me take care of our parents. I need you to help me get through this!" Jennifer stood looking at Scott and slowly calmed her raging emotions. She bent over her brother's beloved face and gently kissed his cheek. Suddenly she felt a newfound strength that was not there just moments before. She dried her eyes and left the room. No one saw her cry after that tearful farewell.

Scott's funeral service reflected a life well lived; over 600 people attended. The Roman Catholic sanctuary could not hold all the people who came to grieve with the family and to celebrate the life of the special person who was Scott Rule. His life had touched so many people! His death reminded them of what had been; it brought into focus the truth of eternity and Scott's new life in heaven.

A couple of weeks after Scott's death, Jennifer lay sleeping, alone in her room. She was lying on her back when something brought her abruptly awake. She opened her eyes to see Scott standing at the foot of her bed! He did not speak; he just stood there quietly, looking directly at Jennifer. Scott was wearing a red, baseball jacket (he had always loved baseball) and dark blue jeans. Both his hands were in his pockets as he stood patiently before her, making sure she knew he was there. Jennifer could not believe what she was seeing. She pulled the bed sheet over her head and closed her eyes. When she opened her eyes again and peered from beneath the sheet, he was no longer present; however, Scott's appearance had made a lasting impression!

Eight years have passed since Scott's accident. Jennifer Dible is now a Nurse Practitioner in Nashville, Tennessee. The passage of time has made reality somewhat less painful, although Jennifer still loves and misses Scott. Looking back, Jennifer says the loss of her brother and the experience of actually seeing him after his death made her faith grow. She remembers: "When I was growing up, going to church was just something you always did. After Scott's death, I became closer to God and my spirituality increased more than I could ever have imagined."

The Rule family accepts Scott's after-death appearance as a special gift from God. The visit left Jennifer with peace of mind and hope; in her words, it is "a very good thing!"

CHAPTER 18

Twice Blessed

Mary Cole was oblivious to the magnificent display out side her bedroom window. When autumn comes to Knoxville, Tennessee, it has the surreal beauty of a picture postcard. During the annual transformation, vibrant rainbows of red, yellow, and orange stretch across the hillsides. But the pain in Mary's heart blinded her to all but the heartbreak of loss.

Mary Cole sat with a Bible in her lap. Only two months before, liver failure had claimed the life of her thirty-two-year-old son, David. The separation was still new to her; time had not yet begun to ease the grief that filled her heart. She found special solace and strength in the Word of God. She had soaked up the Scriptures like a sponge that day, as she diligently sought the Lord and His peace.

Suddenly, Mary became aware she was not alone in her room. She lifted her head to see a very large being sat just in front of her. Mary realized she beheld an angel! It was solid white and sat with its face in its hands, looking at Mary. The entity vanished after a moment; but Mary was certain of what she had seen. The angel had not spoken, but Mary was sure the angel had been sent to comfort her in her time of need. She experienced a profound peace that surrounded her like a warm blanket and her heart was comforted.

Several years passed and Mary's hunger for the Word of God continued unabated. Intense Bible study became a way of life for her and most days found her pouring over God's wonderful Word.

One day, as Mary stood ironing, she felt a presence. She realized a Man stood next to her. His appearance was pure white, from head to toe. No garments accounted for the color; He appeared to be formed of a solid, white matter. She heard no words but knew intuitively the Man was Jesus! He remained for only a few seconds, but long enough for Mary to comprehend the significance of the visitation. Again, as with the angel's appearance, she was engulfed in an overwhelming peace.

Over the years, Mary has remained humbled by, and grateful for, the heavenly visitations. She is quick to acknowledge that her gifts were awesome and sent by God. Mary strongly believes her spirit was open to receive those visits because she had been immersed in the Word of God prior to each. Mary says, "By staying close to and in tune with God, I believe we stay open to direct communication with Him."

CHAPTER 19

Peace

Kathy Dedmon was the Wilson County Building Inspector for many years. She had watched as the sleepy, rural, Tennessee county had changed over the years from a simple, farming community into one of the fastest growing counties in the nation. In early 2009, Kathy retired after a long and successful career. She now takes great pleasure in caring for her grandchild and Kathy never fails to enjoy and appreciate life.

This is Kathy's story.

In April of 1987, Kathy and her husband, Kenneth Ricketts, were living in Watertown, Tennessee. The couple was busy building their lives and making a home for their little family. Without warning, the couple's life together came to an abrupt end. Kenneth suffered a massive heart attack and died in the bedroom of their home. He was only forty years old

Over the next two months, Kathy experienced denial and anger. Each day seemed an eternity.

Grief and confusion so overwhelmed her that Kathy feared for her own sanity. But, there was no escape from the reality and finality of Kenneth's death. Kathy tried to remain strong for her family and, finally, found a degree of acceptance for a circumstance over which she had no control.

One night in early June, Kathy had fallen asleep next to her son in his bed. The six-year-old often had trouble sleeping in the months following his dad's death. To comfort him, Kathy would lie down beside him until he drifted off to sleep. The night was quiet and Kathy and her son had finally fallen into a deep sleep. Suddenly, the sound of someone entering the room awakened Kathy. When she turned to look, a familiar yet disturbing sight met her gaze; Kenneth, her deceased husband, was sitting beside the bed!

Kenneth was wearing a light blue shirt and dark blue pants. He reached out his hand and touched Kathy. She could not feel the touch of his hand, but watched as he gently patted her. Kenneth told her, "Kathy, quit worrying. I'm okay." Then Kenneth was gone. The brevity of his stunning appearance had left Kathy with no time or inclination to respond.

Afterward, Kathy sat quietly in the darkened

room. She contemplated life and death and the separation between the living and the dead. She could not explain or fully understand the visit from her undeniably, dead husband; but she experienced no fear or apprehension. Kathy searched her heart to discover her innermost feelings following the encounter. The only word to describe the calm, gentle acceptance that flooded her being was "peace."

CHAPTER 20

I'm Free

Agnes Johnson lived alone in her Orlando, Florida home. A widow with few friends and no family in the area, Agnes spent many lonely hours. To fill her time, Agnes bought a small, blond-colored organ and set about teaching herself to play. Before long, beautiful music brightened Agnes' small world.

In 1981, Agnes received a wonderful surprise; her niece, Judy was moving to Orlando.

Jim and Judy Johnson were eager to get the move underway. They had wanted to relocate to Orlando for some time and the right job opportunity had paved the way.

Jim, Judy, and their two sons were excited to begin a new chapter in their lives, but ending the old one was difficult. They were saddened to leave their many friends in Wausau, Wisconsin; especially the members of their little, mission church. The members were almost like family, all depending on one another for survival. Preparing for the move was a bittersweet time for the young family.

Once they were settled in their new home, Judy set about getting to know her widowed aunt. Having family live nearby was a novel and welcome change. Their extended family was small, so the Johnsons had always relied heavily on God, faith, and friends to fill their need for love and support. Since they knew no one else in the area, Aunt Agnes represented both friend and family to the transplanted Johnson clan.

Before long, Judy realized Agnes did not attend church services and didn't seem to be affiliated with any of the area's many churches. The fact concerned her, but she kept her thoughts to herself.

Though she did not attend herself, Aunt Agnes urged Jim and Judy to visit St. John's Church. The pastor, Dr. Bob Hawk, had presided at her husband's funeral and had left quite an impression on her. The Johnsons had already visited several churches in the area, each time with no inclination to return; so they quickly agreed to visit St. John's.

Dr. Hawk was on vacation when the Johnsons first visited his church. A member of the congregation acted as a guest speaker. The subject of his sermon was loneliness. The message brought tears to the Johnson's eyes because they desperately missed their Wisconsin home, church family, and friends. They were extremely lonely in their new home and needed to become connected to a new body of believers. Judy remembers, "We were so alone and we just didn't feel needed anymore."

The following Sunday, the Johnson family attended services at St. John's and were pleased to see Dr. Hawk had returned to his pulpit. After hearing him preach, they agreed unanimously that St. John's would be their new church home.

A short time after Judy and Jim moved to Florida, Aunt Agnes developed brain cancer. Judy became her primary caregiver, assisting Agnes as she suffered through the trying ordeal. The cancer progressed rapidly. Agnes endured a craniotomy to remove the tumor and six weeks of agonizing, radiation therapy followed. Agnes' condition deteriorated severely. Realizing Agnes could no longer live at home, Judy facilitated her move to a long-term care facility. Judy lovingly cared for Agnes and fed her the last meal she had on earth before she lapsed into a coma and died in the autumn of 1982.

Following her aunt's death, Judy was plagued by questions. She wondered what happened to Agnes when she died; was Agnes in heaven? Had she done the right thing as a caregiver? Should she have spoken to her aunt about the Lord? At that time, Judy's concept of a Christian was a person who attended church regularly. Since she had never known Aunt Agnes to attend a church service, Judy was not sure where her aunt stood with God. She had always been too hesitant to inquire but had prayed diligently for her critically-ill aunt. Judy longed to know Agnes' fate, but it seemed the answer to that all-important question would never be known.

The only people who came to Agnes' funeral were Jim, Judy, their two sons, and Judy's parents. Before the funeral, Dr. Hawk led them in prayer.

What happened next was simply amazing. The following account is in her own words.

"While we were praying, I saw a vivid picture of Agnes clearly and unmistakably in my spirit and mind! I saw Agnes in an expanse above me, as if she were in a thought bubble above a cartoon. There she was, a few feet above me, seated at her organ, playing music! The organ looked very much like the one she had at her home . . . Her fingers were flying across the keyboard! Her feet were moving on the pedals and she was looking over her shoulder at me! She had the most beautiful smile on her face and she shouted down at me, 'I am free! I'm not locked in this body anymore!' There was color. Her hair had a red tint. In life, she had a round face. In her after-death appearance, her face appeared round and full once again. She was wearing all neutral colors: pale white and light browns. I remember she was wearing a beautiful blouse! I don't remember what her shoes looked like. She looked so pretty—very young, radiant, and healthy! It was almost like looking in a window of heaven!"

All Judy's doubts about Aunt Agnes' destination were dispelled by the incredible display of God's mercy and grace.

After the funeral, church members came to the Johnsons' home, to visit and bring food. Their presence was needed and appreciated by the Johnson family. They formed new relationships; they had finally found a new church home.

Judy's Aunt Agnes was perhaps an isolated, un-churched Christian, but a Christian, none-the-less. Her Godly wisdom guided Jim and Judy to

St. John's Church. Judy says she will always be thankful for the after-death appearance of her Aunt Agnes; it was a very special and very welcome gift from God!

CHAPTER 21

Reunion

Susie Covington Austin lived in Springfield, Tennessee with her husband, Tom (Big Daddy) Austin, until he died in November of 1980, at the age of 66. They had owned and operated Austin Bell Funeral Home for many years.

In 2004, at the age of 85, Susie suffered a heart attack and never fully recovered. She wanted to remain in her home but was too weak to care for herself. Susie's daughter, Marcia Echols, and her granddaughter, Susan Echols, agreed to take turns staying with her. Both of them lived in Nashville at the time.

Marcia knew her mother was a Christian by the way she had lived her life. They had discussed salvation and Susie was confident she would one day enjoy God's presence in heaven. However, Marcia struggled to let her mother go. She prayed, "Oh God, I need confirmation about my mother. The most important thing in the world to me is that all my family will be up there in heaven. That's all that really matters."

Following that prayer, Susie had an extraordinary dream. When she awoke, she realized she had been to heaven! In a voice filled with obvious excitement, she told her daughter, "Guess who was waiting for me at the gate? Big Daddy and Jesus! Big Daddy said, 'I thought you would never get here! I've been waiting for you!' It was wonderful to see him. Then we all went inside and I saw Mama and Papa and many loved ones!"

Susan asked her grandmother if the streets of heaven were really made of gold. Susie replied, "Susan, there was gold everywhere! I saw what looked like pearls. It was so beautiful I cannot even describe it. I am convinced I was really there—in heaven!" Marcia was certain her dream was the confirmation she had requested. She was finally able to release her mother into God's loving care.

On the weekend before Susie's death, the Lord gave Marcia an inner certainty that her mother's earthly life was about to come to a close. And it appeared her mother was also aware of her imminent death. Susie's strength seemed to rally throughout the weekend. She called many of her friends and relatives for brief conversations, telling each of them "goodbye" and assuring them of her love. Susan and her grandmother stayed awake most of Sunday night, reminiscing of days gone by.

On Monday afternoon, Susan left her grandmother's home at 5:00 and Marcia arrived at 5:30. Susie died in that thirty-minute span of time, while she was alone. When Marsha arrived, she found her mom in bed, her upper body elevated and arms extended. Marcia said, "From her position, I would say she saw someone and reached out to go with that person. She was still reaching out when I found her." Marcia gently repositioned her mother's still body into a reclining position.

Marcia recalls, "Mother died the week of Thanksgiving and was buried that weekend. It was a sad holiday without her, but all her family was so thankful to God for blessing us with a godly mother. Many family members and friends came to the funeral to celebrate her life. Mother experienced her own reunion in heaven with all her loved ones from past generations!"

Susie Austin realized dying is a natural part of life; and she faced it alone, sure of the reward to come. For her, death held no fear or pain. Death is only painful to the ones who are left behind.

CHAPTER 22

The Little People

The temperature was 88 degrees and the sky was clear and blue. As Ruby drove through the streets of Orlando, Florida, it seemed she was taking a trip through paradise. Her mood was cheerful and she was thoroughly enjoying the day. She had just left her optometrist's office with a good report; all was right in her world.

Both of Ruby's parents had died years before. Her father, Ernest Ash, had died from cancer in 1997, and her mom, Opal, died of complications from Parkinson's disease in 1999. The couple had been openly affectionate throughout their long life together; their enduring love for one another had been obvious.

Ruby had cared for her mother after her father's death. Feeling helpless, she could only watch as the Parkinson's disease ravaged her mother's body. Near the end, the disease progressed to the point where Opal's breathing was severely impaired. Ruby couldn't bear seeing her mother suffer. Watching her struggle just to breathe was heartrending. She reminded her mom that heaven was waiting; and so was her husband. Opal passed away filled with the hope of being reunited with her beloved Ernest.

Ruby's thoughts were far from her deceased parents on that beautiful, spring day; nothing could have prepared her for what was about to take place.

Suddenly, without warning, Ruby's mom and dad appeared in the car with her! They looked just as Ruby remembered them, except for one major detail: they were small enough to fit onto the dashboard of the car! They sat silently between the steering wheel and the windshield, directly in front of Ruby's awestruck eyes! Opal was wearing a floral, print dress with a black background. Ernest wore a white shirt and dark pants. Opal sat on a chair resembling a stool and Ernest stood behind her with his hands on her shoulders. They were both smiling!

Surprisingly, Ruby was not frightened; the extraordinary occurrence seemed, somehow, perfectly normal. She eagerly spoke to her mom, "Hi Mom! I've been missing you. I love you!" Next she spoke to her dad, "Daddy! I love you, too!" Her parents just smiled up at her, without speaking a single word.

As suddenly as the two appeared, they disappeared! Ruby continued her drive home with a sense of joy and awe.

The incident took place approximately eight years ago, but the details remain vivid in Ruby's mind. Prior to the experience, she would not have believed such a thing possible. But Ruby's faith increased and she has been encouraged by her parents' visit. When asked to sum up the incident in one sentence, Ruby slowly shook her head, smiled, and said "What a gift from God!"

CHAPTER 23

A Mother's Love

In early 2009, Chuck Fuller began to complain of chest pains and an irregular heart beat. Never one to allow much to stand in his way, Chuck attributed his health problems to the pressure he was under at work and kept going, full-speed ahead. Trip Supreme, a very successful travel agency, was Chuck's pride and joy. Owning the business was rewarding but had proven to be incredibly stressful at times.

Adding to the stress was a giant portion of grief and confusion that defined much of Chuck's life. He had experienced many painful emotions since his mother, Debbie Davis, had died at the young age of 49.

Debbie had made some regrettable choices in her life that had negatively affected her relationship with Chuck. Most of Chuck's life was spent separated from his mother and his grandparents had assumed primary responsibility for raising him and his sister. For as long as he could remember,

Chuck had been at odds within himself where his mother was concerned. He loved her, but hated the affect her choices had on her family. Chuck had longed for a loving, close relationship with his mother, but over the years, that relationship had remained a dream, never a reality. It wasn't until the last two years of his mother's life that they were able to develop a semblance of the relationship Chuck craved.

One spring night in 2009, Chuck was awakened at three o'clock in the morning by severe chest pain and an alarmingly, abnormal heartbeat. When he collapsed in the hall, his wife Jamie called 911. The ambulance arrived and the paramedics immediately put Chuck on a gurney and wheeled him to the ambulance. The doors were left standing open as they started an IV and placed a nitroglycerin tablet under Chuck's tongue. As he laid on the gurney, Chuck wondered if death was near. His eyes searched about fearfully, as if looking for an answer.

Suddenly, through the open ambulance doors, Chuck saw an unimaginably bright, white light! In the midst of the light, Chuck could see his mom's face!

Chuck remembers, "She was just standing there

at the back of the ambulance, watching me."

Chuck saw only the upper portion of Debbie's body. In life, she had suffered from a condition that caused the muscles on one side of her face to droop. Chuck recalls that her younger-looking, beautiful face glowed; all evidence of the disfiguring condition was gone. Debbie looked absolutely radiant and the picture of health.

Debbie stood looking at her son, tears filling her eyes and spoke one word, repeating it compassionately, "No, no, no." Chuck somehow knew his mother was saying "no" to his death; she was telling him to live. Her countenance was that of a loving mother, tenderly caring for a beloved child. Chuck interpreted her tears as tears of joy, tears from a grateful soul that had found the right road home. Chuck finally felt loved by his mother and his heart was filled with hope and peace! He understood it was not time for him to leave this life. As the realization took hold in Chuck's mind, Debbie slowly faded from his sight.

Chuck was taken to Summit Medical Center in Hermitage, Tennessee for treatment and experienced a full recovery.

Chuck is certain his mother is in heaven. He believes she came at that crucial time in his life to demonstrate her love for him and encourage him to live; and quite possibly, to save his life!

CHAPTER 24

Peaceful Valley

Bill Sims was a strong and rugged man, inside and out. Through most of his difficult life, he recognized no need for God or His church. Though his wife was a godly woman with a strong faith, Bill preferred to rely on his own strength. His independent attitude continued unchanged after he suffered a near fatal, work-related accident that left him wheelchair bound for ten years. Now permanently crippled and cane dependent, Bill remained hardened to God's truth even after cancer claimed the life of his son.

Bill was an Ohio native who had moved his family to Florida. Soon after his son's death, Bill decided to return to his hometown for a Christmas visit. Bill's physician advised him to forego the trip. Winters in Ohio are brutally cold and damp and the doctor was concerned Bill's compromised physical condition would put him at risk for respiratory problems in the harsh, northern climate. True to form, Bill refused to accept his doctor's warning and was soon on his way to enjoy an Ohio Christmas with his family.

After only a few days in the Ohio, winter weather, Bill became extremely ill. He was diagnosed with pneumonia and admitted to the hospital in serious condition. Despite continuous medical attention, Bill's pneumonia worsened. For several days, his physicians fought to save his life. For a brief time, it seemed they would lose the battle — Bill appeared to be more dead than alive.

Bill's physicians were successful in saving his life and Bill recovered from the life-threatening pneumonia. But Bill's life would never be the same. As Bill's doctors fought to save Bill's physical life, Bill had encountered the reality of spiritual existence.

At some point during Bill's battle with pneumonia, Bill had visited a different world. He remembers seeing a peaceful valley carpeted with lush, green grass. It was an incredibly beautiful place with towering, elegant trees. As Bill gazed at the idyllic scene, he saw his son walking toward him. A brilliant, white light surrounded him as he approached his dad. His son spoke a simple message in a clear, sure voice, "Go back, Dad. Go back! It's not time for you to come here yet; you have more work to do!"

Bill recovered completely and returned to Florida where he lived for many more years. After his near-death experience, the things of God seemed to have new meaning for him. The experience gave Bill a new perspective on living and dying that lead him to find salvation through Jesus Christ. Bill was a changed man with a new and tender heart. He found solace and truth through his son's appearance from the other side.

When Bill died many years after his near-death experience, no one doubted he was a saved man who had simply finished his journey on earth and moved on to his heavenly home!

A fictitious name was used to protect the identity of the deceased.

CHAPTER 25

Miraculous Trilogy

PART ONE

Although the Vietnam War still raged abroad, Danny Kellum enlisted in the Army immediately after he graduated from college. Soon after completing Officer Candidate School, he was ordered to active duty in Vietnam. Danny was a newly wed and struggled to tell his young wife he would soon be leaving. His wife feared he would die in combat, but Danny was committed and courageous. He came from a long line of patriots; he was ready to serve his country, no matter the cost.

Danny's company was deployed. Danny served as a Forward Observer for the 101st Airborne Division, assigned to Alpha Company, the second of the 502nd Infantry. Their mission was "search and destroy." This meant they were sent into a particular area by helicopter with orders to destroy the enemy before the enemy destroyed them. Fear and anxiety were constant companions for Alpha

Company and its Forward Observer.

With incredible clarity, Danny recalls a particular mission. Alpha Company had been in the same location for ten days, a strange departure from protocol, which required relocation every 24 hours. Danny remembers, "We were in the mountainous jungles of South Vietnam; securing a location that overlooked the Song Bo River. During that time, we were interdicting enemy concentration in the area. Through intercepted enemy communication, we discovered that our position was going to be overrun by the enemy that night." Alpha company would have to move out.

Believing there were enemy soldiers just outside the area, Danny's platoon waited for darkness to begin the search for a safe place to spend the night. No flashlights aided their search; they navigated through the black night with only the guide of a compass. Unable to locate an elevated place where gravity would make defense easier (it is a much simpler task to throw hand grenades down hill), they took refuge in a low-lying area.

Later that evening, an artillery barrage was mounted against the recently vacated location, now overrun by the enemy. The night was pitch black making accurate targeting of the area nearly impossible. In an effort to direct the artillery, a smoke round from World War II was fired into the air above the vicinity of the enemies' location. Both rounds failed to explode and crashed to the earth. Although Danny could not see the smoke, he heard the round's impact. Using the sound as his guide, Danny fired two rounds of high explosives toward the target. One round went off unexpectedly close. The explosion was only a few feet away from where Danny and his troops were located; however, Danny and his troops were totally unscathed.

Danny says, "I still don't know what happened that night but that round almost killed us." As Danny relates the circumstances of his brush with death, it is obvious he is convinced that only divine intervention saved his life.

MIRACULOUS TRILOGY: PART TWO

Two days later, Danny's platoon had made its' way to a clearing atop a hill, a makeshift Landing

Zone (LZ) for helicopters. From that position, Danny began to shoot artillery toward the enemies' location.

"As I stood there, I heard a piece of shrapnel coming at us," said Danny. "A bullet makes a whistling sound; shrapnel makes a chirping sound. You can't see shrapnel coming anymore than you can see a bullet coming at you; they move at the same speed. It was singing through the air. I decided to stand very still and let it miss me. It did not miss me. It hit me in the heart . . . area of my chest! I was knocked on the ground . . . it cut and bruised me but it did not kill me."

Later Danny held the piece of shrapnel up against his chest and had his radiotelephone operator (RTO) take a picture. The shrapnel was almost five inches long and nearly two inches wide; a jagged hunk of metal that looked like it was ripped from a solid sheet of steel. Mistakenly, the roll of film containing the photo was sent to his wife. She wrote Danny asking what that was in his hand against his chest. He neglected to answer her question in his next letter. Only when he was safely home did he tell her the real story about how God saved him from certain death!

Danny now recalls, "If that piece of shrapnel

had been turned another fraction of an inch, or had I moved another fraction of an inch; if I had tried to dodge a fraction of an inch it would have gone through me and taken out my heart and lungs, instantly!"

"I reached down and picked it up then got down on my knees and thanked God for sparing my life. As a believer, I knew that I was alive because God Himself had protected me; He had positioned me perfectly still. Then He positioned that piece of shrapnel in such a way that it broad sided me instead of slicing through me." Danny has never doubted that, once again, divine intervention protected him from death.

MIRACULOUS TRILOGY: PART THREE

It has been thirty-nine years since Danny Kellum began his tour of duty in the Army. Second Lt. Danny Kellum is now Dr. Kellum; He serves as the Head Master of Donelson Christian Academy, a private Christian school in Nashville, Tennessee.

His lifestyle now is much different from the life threatening conditions of an Artillery Forward Observer. God's protective love is still active in Dr. Kellum's life; divine intervention is still a fact in this grateful man's experience.

A few years ago, Dr. Kellum was assisting in the disassembly of a large scaffold that had been used during graduation to hold a huge drapery. One piece of scaffolding had been disengaged and lowered to the ground. Dr. Kellum worked to loosen the next section. Suddenly, he lost his footing and fell twenty-four feet to the gymnasium floor! His body struck the scaffolding many times before he landed heavily, his back and head crashing with great force into the solid, wooden surface.

Dr. Kellum remained conscious after the fall. He even remembers hearing a student call 911for assistance. He was taken by ambulance to the emergency room of Vanderbilt Medical Center. Dr. Kellum was thoroughly examined due to the distance and impact of his fall. A number of scrapes and bruises were found, but Dr. Kellum had miraculously escaped any serious injury. He walked out of the emergency room that same day!

"It was a miraculous event from God," said Dr. Kellum. His life had been spared once again.

MIRACULOUS TRILOGY: EPILOGUE

Dr. Kellum is able to look back over the past 39 years with genuine gratitude toward God, still giving Him all the glory for each time his life has been spared.

Dr. Kellum has two sons and a daughter, Deeannah; Dan is presently in the Tennessee Air National Guard and Rob is in the US Army. Both men have served one tour in Iraq and Rob will soon be deployed to Afghanistan. The advice Dr. Kellum has offered his sons is this: "Be faithful and true to God. Make sure you share your faith with others. There will always be people who are looking and searching for answers to life and life's questions; Jesus is the answer. Others need to hear . . . your testimony to be able to fully understand your relationship to God. Do not think people will observe your lives and see Jesus. You must share the gospel."

CHAPTER 26

What Do You Believe?

Pastor Alton Parker was a Missionary Baptist minister from a small, rural town near Nashville, Tennessee. He was a godly man, sincerely devoted to serving the Lord. He was highly regarded and respected by his parishioners.

Without warning, Pastor Parker suffered a stroke that left him severely impaired. Following extensive tests, it was discovered Pastor Parker had a significant blockage of the right carotid artery, the main blood vessel leading to the right side of the brain. Since the right side of the brain controls the left side of the body, the stroke had left Pastor Parker with his left side paralyzed; hopefully, a temporary condition.

Dr. Arthur Cushman, a neurosurgeon in Nashville, recommended Pastor Parker undergo a carotid endarterectomy, a procedure to remove the fatty buildup of plaque from his carotid artery. Pastor Parker agreed and was admitted to the hospital for the procedure.

The surgery was uneventful and the surgery team prepared to take Pastor Parker to post-operative care. They had just disconnected the anesthetic when Pastor Parker's blood pressure began to climb to a potentially lethal level. Fearing a brain hemorrhage would result, the anesthetist quickly administered intravenous medication to lower Pastor Parker's dangerous blood pressure. The medication worked too well. His pressure dropped to zero and his heart nearly stopped. The operating team worked frantically, giving him CPR (cardiopulmonary resuscitation), and successfully resuscitated him. Pastor Parker survived and suffered no ill effects from the surgery.

The next day in the intensive care unit, Pastor Parker requested a private conversation with Dr. Cushman. The nurse left the room and he proceeded with a question: "I died at the end of the surgery, didn't I?" He continued, "My soul floated out of my body and I watched as the resuscitation was going on." Reverend Parker was able to accurately and precisely describe the series of events that had taken place. He told Dr. Cushman exactly where he and each member of the operating team was standing and what they said during those critical moments. The accuracy of his account stunned and amazed Dr. Cushman.

"I traveled through a long dark tunnel where I had a review of my entire life!" said Pastor Parker. "When I reached the end of the tunnel, I approached a beautiful bright light and a beautiful land! I saw Jesus and the angels. I saw many of my family members who died years ago. All of my loved ones looked very young and vigorous. Brilliant, white light surrounded each individual! My deceased loved ones came to greet me and it was like a family reunion! It was all so wonderful; I just wanted to stay there. I came back only because Jesus told me I had to. He said it was not time for me to die."

Accompanied by angels, the Pastor returned to his body and woke up in the recovery room. When he awoke, he felt wonderful and filled with extreme peace. He was no longer afraid of dying.

Pastor Parker told Dr. Cushman, "My church does not believe this can happen. They believe there is no separation of body, soul, and spirit. They believe all die together and await the resurrection when Jesus comes back." Pastor Parker had no idea how he would tell his church about his near-death experience.

Dr. Cushman then took his hand and said,

"Thank you, Brother Parker. What do you believe?" In answer, Pastor Parker just smiled an all-knowing smile, quite confident about what had happened to him and where he had been!

A fictitious name was used to protect the identity of the patient.

CHAPTER 27

Changed

At the age of 76, Kelly Turner received a startling diagnosis: he was in the final stage of lung cancer. A kind and simple man who had grown up in the country, Mr. Turner was seriously ill at ease in city settings and detested hospitals. However, he wisely decided to overcome his hesitance; he was admitted to the hospital in Oak Ridge, Tennessee for chemotherapy.

Understandably, Mr. Turner struggled with the knowledge of his impending death. He had many visitors and enjoyed their company, but the dire prognosis caused a pall to overshadow every visit.

Before Mr. Turner's chemotherapy could begin, it was necessary for minor surgery to be performed to insert an access port into an artery. Mr. Turner was lightly sedated during the procedure; he tolerated it well and there were no complications. After the completion of the procedure, Mr. Turner was brought back to his room. It was obvious that something about him had changed!

After the procedure, Mr. Turner's sad, somber countenance was replaced by a joyous attitude! Mr. Turner smiled a radiant smile; he seemed overjoyed and elated! When his family questioned him about the change that had come over him, Mr. Turner explained, "I have been with Jesus! He told me I am going to be alright and everything is going to be okay!"

Mr. Turner told his family he had visited heaven during the surgical procedure; he had seen Jesus! He reported having seen many deceased loved ones during his time with the Lord; strangely, he had also seen his daughter, Virginia.

Virginia was quite obviously alive and well, and found her father's report quite perplexing. Though her dad was certain of the reality of his near-death encounter, Virginia struggled to understand her own presence in the vision. Being prone to worry and anxiety, Virginia found herself a bit uneasy. Finally, she came to realize her dad had actually seen into the future—to a time when they would, indeed, be together in the kingdom of God.

Mr. Turner's near-death encounter left him with a lasting euphoria. He maintained his good spirits throughout his remaining days. Mr. Turner died one month after his heavenly vision.

Virginia had been especially close to her dad and found it extremely hard to deal with his death. She spent many sleepless nights, struggling to find peace and acceptance.

One night, about a week after her father's death, Virginia failed to find much-needed sleep. As she lay in bed, wide awake, her father appeared in her bedroom. He was only a couple of feet away, leaning against the dresser close to the foot of her bed. He was wearing jeans and a golden-tan, striped shirt. He looked vibrant and healthy!

Mr. Turner spoke to his daughter, "Gin, you need to stop worrying and don't be afraid. It is alright to acknowledge the things that bother you; however, you must learn to let those things go." As suddenly as he appeared, he vanished.

Virginia turned the light on and got out of the bed, reasoning with herself about what she had just experienced. She was not dreaming; she was wide-awake. Though she could not explain the strange occurrence, she was not upset or frightened. Her worry and anxiety seemed to have evaporated; she was no longer concerned about her dad!

After her father's visit, Virginia began to experience a new found peace; not only was her concern about her father gone, she discovered her predisposition to worry and fret had quieted and her fearful heart had stilled. It seemed quite clear to Virginia that her dad's after-death appearance was an attempt to impart a message to her. Was he trying to say, "Hold onto faith, let go of fear?"

In the time that has passed since her dad's visit Virginia has learned to release fear and worry, maintaining a calm, trusting, inner confidence. She came away from the experience with the certain knowledge of God's love and presence and an enduring sense of peace.

Epilogue

Beyond the world in which we live, there exists a spiritual one filled with the unknown and the inexplicable. Divine intervention is not uncommon. Near-death and after-death experiences happen every day. Sometimes referred to as "paranormal" or "supernatural," these extraordinary events are actually God's miraculous intervention into the lives of those He loves. God is not silent and He is not distant from His people.

His messages of hope are still heard by listening ears and miracles still occur in the lives of those with expectant faith. He reveals His presence in life-changing events and in the smallest details of every day life! When His miracles are demonstrated, we are filled with hope and encouragement!

I believe God is honored and glorified when we tell of the great things He has done, when we tell of His wondrous works.

Miraculous occurrences remind us that God is real! He knows each of us by name. He knows everything about us: intimate details, silent thoughts, and deepest desires. He created us; so He understands why we are the way we are.

When something miraculous happens, the believer is encouraged and filled with everlasting hope. We are strengthened and reminded that we are never alone, even in the worst of times. We are enticed to focus our minds on the things above instead of the temporal things on earth. Heaven is our real home and our lives are put in proper perspective when we realize God is in control.

Extraordinary and unexplainable circumstances beckon to hearts that instinctively yearn for God, even before the brain is willing to acknowledge Him. A mighty miracle awaits every single human being on earth! It is the miracle of salvation, a free gift to you and to me. Jesus was crucified and died on the cross; He paid the cost of the miracle!

I am still amazed by the fact that God loved me enough to send his Son, Jesus, to die on a cross — to buy my pardon — so I may spend eternity in heaven! I have lived with God and I have lived without Him; living without Him is not living at all. I remember when I asked Jesus to come into my heart and the internal changes that followed. The words 'Thank You" never seem adequate. The only way I know to thank Him properly is to live the rest of my life here on earth sharing with others what He has done for me.

From personal experience, I know these things: if we call to Him, He hears us; if we believe He hears us, He will answer us. He is always ready and willing to love and forgive us if we will only ask Him. No soul is irretrievable and God can right any wrong on earth. All things are possible with God!

Prayer is our way of speaking to God. The Bible is God's way of speaking to us. When we commune with God and God with us, a relationship is born. When we confess our sins and ask Jesus into our hearts, forgiveness is granted and salvation is bestowed by God's mercy and grace. God is always reaching out to each of us!

God sends His miracles to awaken us from sleep so we can see His lovely smile and hear His amazing voice! Remember, He is not far away but here, today, longing for each of His children to whisper, "Father, I need You". I promise you, He will answer, "Here I am."

Author's Afterword

I am very interested in hearing from readers who would care to share their near-death experiences, after-death appearances or messages, angel encounters, miraculous answers to prayer and stories of divine intervention. You may contact me at Stories@DavisJacksonPublishers.com. If I am able to use your story in a future book, I will contact you for permission.

If you have comments regarding this book, go to: FaxFromHeaven@DavisJacksonPublishers.com.

Faye Aldridge